The Apparel and Uniform of the Order of Saint Lazarus throughout the ages

Charles Savona-Ventura

Malta
2020

Publishers: Lulu Ltd, U.S.A.
ISBN: 978-0-244-86811-6

Contents

FOREWORD 5

THE MEDIEVAL APPAREL OF THE LAZARITE KNIGHTS.............................7

THE UNIFORMS OF SAINT LAZARUS DURING THE BAROQUE AND MODERN PERIODS

....27

THE FEMALE DRESS OF THE ORDER 41

THE EIGHT-POINTED BREAST CROSS..47

THE HISTORY OF HERALDRY WITHIN THE ORDER 65

DRESS CODE PROTOCOL 89

Foreword

A Chivalric Order requires its members to dress appropriately according to the occasion and according to established current dress regulations defining the percieved unifom of the organization. The Order of Saint Lazarus throughout the ages has included provisions within its statutes to define what the dress code or "uniform" of its members should be.

These statutory regulations reflected the percieved charisma or role of the Order within the society it was working in, ranging from enforcing a monkish-style habit for its members in the early centuries, becoming more gentry and eventually military in style as the role of the Order within society changed. The military style generally followed the military dress fashion of the time.

This booklet aims to review the history of the development of the Order's dress code, uniforms, and insignia. It further defines the present-day dress regulations with simple instructions on what is appropriate wear in different circumstances.

The Medieval apparel of the Lazarite knights

Abstract

The Order of Saint Lazarus saw its origins as a monastic hospitaller order but adopted a military role. The apparel of the early members was one emulating the monastic medicament orders adopting their respective rules. They however had to further have attire provisions in war adopting the armour prevalent at the time. The monastic links were slowly and gradually put aside, and the Order assumed the role of a landowning organization managed by non-religious gentry-members of the Order changing the general attire of the members.

Introduction

In the 1599, William Shakespeare wrote the play *Hamlet* set in the late middle ages in Denmark. In Act 1 Scene 3 of the play, Polonius instructs his son Laertes how to comport himself and instructs him: 'Costly thy habit as thy purse can buy, but not expressed in fancy—rich, not gaudy, for the apparel oft proclaims the man, and they in France of the best rank and station are of a most select and generous chief in that.'[1] The clothes one wore during the Medieval Period were certainly an important indicator of the status of the person wearing them. Like everything else, the Feudal System established a Pyramid of Power that influenced all aspects of life including clothing and fashion for the different social classes. By the late 13th century in some European countries, this was further regulated by Sumptuary Laws [e.g. the English Sumptuary Laws of 1281]. Medieval peasant clothing was basic and practical, consisting of breeches generally made of leather, doublets, and a capes of coarse brown wool. The tunic was tied at the waist by a belt, to which a knife, purse, and sometimes working tools were suspended. The nobiliary wore

---

[1] William Shakespeare. *Hamlet*. Act 1 scene 3 line 70.

more luxurious clothing that identified and ranked them to their social class.

The monastic movement transcended all social classes since all individuals joining a monastic order were obliged to wear a common attire specific to the order they were joining. Monasticism required the individual to renounce all worldly pursuits to devote oneself fully to spiritual work some providing a medicament service to the poor and needy. The majority of medicament orders initially followed the Rule of Saint Benedict of Nursia, though in the 13th century many adopted the simpler Rule of Saint Augustine due to its relative brevity. The First Crusade was to see the development of a different form of monastic orders – orders that adopted medicament, hospitaller and military role initially mainly directed towards pilgrims to the Holy Land. These military hospitaller orders in the Outremer initially included the Templars, the Hospitallers, and the Lazarities. These orders embraced members from all sections of society and had different levels of membership. In common with monastic principles, the different rules adopted required a common simple attire. Chapter 55 of the Rule of St. Benedict says clothing was to be adequate and suited to the climate and locality, at the discretion of the abbot. It must be as plain and cheap as was consistent with due economy. Each monk was to have a change of clothes to allow for washing, and when travelling was to have clothes of better quality. Old clothes were to be given to the poor.[2]

Monk's dress

The 12th-13th century dress of the members of the Order of Saint Lazarus is not depicted anywhere. A dedicated rule for the Order of Saint Lazarus was only drawn up during the twelfth century and appears to have closely emulated the Rule of the Temple. The earliest extant copy of this Rule is a copy drawn up in the early decades of the fourteenth century after had adopted the Rule of Saint Augustine (before 1254) and after it had been expelled from the Outremer (in 1291). These regulations clearly

---

[2] Benedict of Nursia. *St. Benedict's Rule for Monasteries*. Minnesota: Order of St. Benedice, 1948, pp.6-7.

emphasise the strong monastic character of the community but confirm that, like the Order of the Temple, the Lazarite community embraced various different types of membership. They also recommend reference to the Rules of the Templars and of the Hospitallers for further guidance whenever necessary.

The 14th century statutes of the Order of Saint Lazarus detail the dress form of the members: 'the monk's habits, which are riding habits, should be made of camel hair or other warming material and should be non-secular; at the front, there should be a green cross, the width of an outstretched hand, with a link along one side and a slightly shorter bar that passes above. However, on the uniform jackets and on the shields, a larger cross has to be worn by brothers fighting in battle in the Holy Land; also, on the banner, there is a large cross. At other times, when there is peace, the brothers shall go out for rides in riding coats. But during worship and when at the table or when simply walking around, they shall go in mantles that are cut respectably and clerically, from camel-hair cloth that is not too valuable but also not of too low quality. However, during the summer, they shall wear thin mantles with clasps that are not cut out at the back, and on the left side there will be a green cross attached lengthwise in the way described above for the monk's habits. The other gowns are the tunics, and the confrères shall not have overcoats cut according to worldly custom. The overcoats should rather be at the front without V-shaped extensions, of a suitable length at the front and the lower tunics should be equipped with belts. However, fur tunics and furs, as well as bed covers, shall only be made from sheepskin or goatskin. Trousers shall be white or black, not valuable and without attached feet; and trousers made of leather shall be worn when one must ride. And at other times, shoes shall neither be laced nor equipped with rings nor poulaine-style but shall instead be cut appropriately.'[3]

---

[3] Siegfried von Schlatt. *Dei Regein des Heiligen Orderns S. Lazari*. Ms. Seedorf Monastery. Ms. 1314/31. Transcribed and translated in: Charles Savona-Ventura [editor]. *Die Regül deß Heiligen Ordens S. Lazari 1314/1321 zu 1418 - The Rules of the Holy Order of S. Lazarus 1314/1321 to 1418*. Lulu Ltd., U.S.A., 2020.

It is generally assumed that the Lazarite Order, extant in the Outremer by the 11th century,[4] originally followed the Rule of St. Benedict. The earliest Benedictine monks wore habits of un-dyed white or grey wool. However, as time went by, black became the prevailing colour. The habits consisted of a tunic tied around the waist with a cloth or leather belt. A scapula consisting of a long wide piece of woollen cloth worn over the shoulders with an opening for the head was worn over the tunic. The front of the scapula was secured with a small piece of rectangular cloth that snapped the sides together. A cowl or hood was attached to the scapula.

Benedictine monks[5]

During the Crusader Period, the Order of St. Lazarus had a close relationship of the Order with the Order of the Temple and thus it is assumed that the Lazarite monks and knights had adopted similar dress regulations to that of the Order of the Temple. The Templar Rule commanded 'that all the brothers' habits should always be of one colour,

---

[4] Charles Savona-Ventura. A Hospitalis infirmorum Sancti Lazari de Jerusalem before the First Crusade. *Acta Historiae Sancti Lazari Ordinis*, 2017, 2:pp.13-26.
[5] *St. Benedict delivering his Rule to St. Maurus and other monks of his order.* Painting in the Monastery of St. Gilles, Nimes (France), 1129.

Augustinian monk

that is white or black or brown. And we grant to all knight brothers in winter and in summer if possible, white cloaks; ...... But these robes should be without any finery and without any show of pride ...'.[6] The Templar knights differentiated themselves by wearing a red Crusader cross insignia; the Lazarite knights wore a green cross.

By 1255, the Order of Saint Lazarus was placed under the rule of Saint Augustine.[7] One may assume that the Lazarite monks then adopted the dress of this religious monastic Order which aimed to 'not be ostentatious, nor shall you wish to please because of the garments you wear but because of your good morals',[8] reflecting the Augustinian Rule to 'avoid singularity in dress and strive to please others by your conduct and not by your clothes.[9] The choir and

---

[6] J.M. Upton-Ward, *The Rule of the Templars*. Woodbridge: Boydell Press, 2005, p.24.

[7] The Order of Saint Lazarus was confirmed by Pope Alexander IV as an *Ordinum Fratrum & Militul Hospitalis Leprosorum S. Lazari Hierosolymitani sub Regula S. Augustini* on the 11 April 1255. See papal bull *Cum á nob is petitur.....* In: L. Cherubini & A.M. Cherubino. *Magnum bullarium romanum, a B. Leone Magno vsque as S.D.N. Inncocentium X*. Lyon: P. Borde, L. Arnaud & C.I. Rigad, 1727, vol.1, p.106.

On 15 July 1255, Pope Alexander IV issued the bull *Cum quaedam salubria* to command a number of religious groupings to gather for the purpose of being amalgamated into a new Order of Hermits of Saint Augustine. The delegates from other small religious communities met in Rome on 1 March 1256, which resulted in a union. Lanfranc Septala of Milan, Prior of the Bonites, was appointed the first prior general of the newly constituted Order. The belted, black tunic of the Tuscan hermits was adopted as the common religious habit.

[8] Siegfried von Schlatt, 1314/31, *op. cit.*

[9] *The Rule of Saint Augustine*. www.op.org/domcentral/trad/default.htm

outdoor dress of the Augustinian friars is a tunic of black woollen material, with long, wide sleeves, a black leather girdle and a large shoulder cape to which is attached a long, pointed hood reaching to the girdle.[10]

The first depiction of the dress used by members of the Order dates to

**Thomas de Sainville
(died 1312)**

the early fourteenth century in the form of a tombstone depiction of Thomas de Sainville (died 1312) who served as a *maître* of the Order. Here, the master is depicted as wearing a sombre long round-necked cloak laced with a collar and charged with the cross of the Order on the left shoulder. The garments beneath are depicted as being similar to a monkish long garment with buttoned sleeves, fastened by a heavy belt very much in the Augustinian tradition. A similar habit was worn by other fourteenth century-serving *maîtres* including Jean de Paris (died 1349) and Jacques de Besses (died 1384) whose tombstone effigies were also recorded.[11]

---

[10] *St Nicholas of Tolentino*. Painting by Piero della Francesca 133 x 60 cm oil and tempera on panel, Museo Poldi Pezzoli, Milan (Italy), c.1460.

[11] Tombeaux de Thomas de Sainville, Jean de Paris et Jacques de Baine, maîtres de l'Ordre de Saint-Lazare de Jérusalem (gravures). *Recueil de pièces, extraits, mémoires et documents concernant les Ordres de Saint-Lazare et du Mont-Carmel. I.* Paris: Ms. Bibliothèque nationale de France, Département des manuscrits, Clairambault 1316.

Raimondo de Bolera
(lived c.1297)

The preference towards depicting deceased members of the Crusader Orders as wearing a sombre monk's habit on their tombstone effigies during the 13th century was common to the all these Orders. This is exemplified by the tombstone belonging to Raimondo di Bolera who served as the preceptor to the *domus Sancte Marie de Suberito*.[12] The inscribed text around this tombstone reads:

⬛*Hic Iacet F(rate)r Ramundus De Bolera Preceptor Olim Domus Sancte Marie De Suberito Anima Eius Requiescat In Pace*

An original Templar link for Raimondo de Bolera is presumed because of the *agnus dei* (Pascal lamb) *reguardant* symbol in the left shield. The shield on the right side depicting a sheep *rampant* facing right may represent the coat-of-arms of the de Bolera family. Raimondo is shown wearing a monk's habit with a cape depicting the Templar Cross on the left breast. Raimondo is reported to have in 1297 ratified a previous deed of sale dated 1219 with which Abbess Giacoma and two other nuns of the monastery of S. Maria a Mare di Barletta sold to Fra 'Trasmundo, tutor of S. Maria di Sovereto, «*una petiam terrae quae est in the Terlitii estate* ». The church of S. Maria di Sovereto is mentioned for the first time in an *acta mortis causa* of 1175

---

[12] Maurizio lo Conte. *La ricerca del Santo Graal nel Mezzogiorno d'Italia. Volume Secondo – Milites Christi*. Lulu Ltd., U.S.A., 2012, p.95. Vincenzo d'Aere. *Sovereto, simbolismo Templare e verità taciute*. Hera, 2001, 23: pp.46-50. The alternative suggestion is that Raimondo di Bolera was a member of the Order of Saint John of Jerusalem.

when a certain Elijah, disposing *pro anima*, imposed on his two heirs – the brothers Pietro and Plancarotta - a substantial bequest in favour of some churches in the Terlizzese: among these, that of S. Maria " de Suberito ", which suggests that it must have been, for some time, a centre of significant religious interest.[13]

Military apparel

The Crusader knight

The 14th century tomb effigies depict no military endowments, though it would have been expected that the knights in battle would have worn battle attire considered suitable for the era. The main armour protecting the Crusader knight was the mail shirt [*haubergeon*] that consisted of a long metal chainmail shirt with sleeves running down to the wrists. The hands were protected with a set of mail mittens. Underneath the chainmail shirt, the knight wore a quilted coat [*gambeson*] and padded trousers [*chausses*]. Over the leg paddings, chain mail leggings were buckled on. Spurs were worn to control the horse. The head was protected by a chainmail hood reaching down to the shoulders. Underneath this, a cloth cap padded the chainmail hood. The head was further protected by a metal "pot" helmet with narrow slots for the eyes. Over the mail shirt, the knight wore a surcoat that had specific marks to identify him to the regiment he was fighting with. The surcoat had the added advantage of keeping the hot desert sun off the metal

---

[13] Paolo Lopane. *I «Templari di s. Giovanni»: La Fondazione monastico-militare di S. Maria di Sovereto*. http://www.lopanepaolo.it/1/contributi_storiografici_1844469.html

armour. The surcoat was belted at the waist helping support the weight of the mail at the hips reducing the weight carried by the shoulders.[14]

By the 15th century the chainmail armour was replaced by metal chest plate armour. It appears that the knights of the Order of Saint Lazarus had adopted chest plate armour by the late 15th century. A sculptured pedestal serving as the base to a statute of Saint Anthony in the Chapel of Saint-Antoine-de-Grattemont, France dated to 1480 depicts a series of six praying members of the Order of Saint Lazarus.[15] The six Lazarites include four knights identified by the helmets placed at their feet and the sword clearly carried by one of them. The other two represented Lazarites are medicament brothers, each carrying a medicament purse and a book of prayers at their feet. The four knights appear to be wearing a cuirass-type armour covering the torso with shoulder vambraces linked to elbow vambraces by a rerebrac. The thighs appear to be protected by tassets and cuisses. A cloak was worn over the armour. The depicted helmets are of the bascinet form with a pointed hounskull or "pig-faced" type visor in use during the fourteenth century.

| Bascinet with hounskull visor - Milan, c.1400 | Plate armour, 15th century |

---

[14] A kneeling knight with his horse before setting off on the crusades. His servant leaning over the turret with his master's helmet. From the *Westminster Psalter*, BL Royal MS 2 A xxii f. 220

[15] Pedestal in Chapel of Saint-Antoine-de-Grattemont, France. Depicted in Raphael Hyacinthe. *L'Ordre de Sant-Lazare de Jerusalem au Moyen Age*. Millau: Conservatoire Larzac Templier et Hospitalier, 2003, pp.134-135.

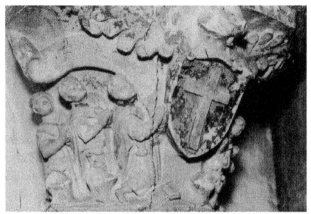

1 ------- 2 ------ 3

4 ----- 5 ---- 6

Pedestal depicting four knights [1-2-4-6] and two religious brothers [3-5]
Chapel of Saint-Antoine-de-Grattemont, France - 1480

The dress of the *fratres hospitalis Sancti Lazari* during the fourteenth to the sixteenth centuries appears to have continued to emulate the simple religious habit of the other monastic orders. A sixteenth-century broadside depicts the Lazarite monk wearing a loose-fitting ankle length tunic and a ferraiolo-type cape. He appears to be wearing a clerical hat over a hood. He holds the leper's clapper in the right hand and a book and shaft in the left. The broadside depicts a dog at the feet of individual, in heraldry signifying loyalty and leadership status in the chivalric order.[16]

16ᵗʰ century broadside showing leper brother holding clapper

---

[16] A sixteenth century broadsheet related to leprosy. Reproduced in J. Harter. *Images of Medicine*. New York: Bonanza books, 1991, 202.

The Reformation and Counter-Reformation movements of the fifteenth-sixteenth centuries brought about a distancing of the Order from the purely medicament and military role adopted in the earlier centuries.[17] The members of the Order became increasingly involved with the military campaigns and the Order assumed the role of a landowning organization managed by non-religious gentry-members of the Order. This change was satirically depicted by a mid-sixteenth century illustration which clearly shows the Lazarite monk changing his dress from the earlier sober monkish habit to the trendy secular clothes of the period. The illustration shows the Lazarite monk to be wearing a dark brown loose-fitting tunic possibly covered by a scapular and cowl. The head is covered by a hood. He carries a leper's clapper in the left hand and a *paternostres* string of fourteen beads in the right. The Lazarite gentry-member is wearing a linen white shirt with a V-necked collar ruff and matching wrist ruffs, which were probably starched to be kept stiff and bright. Over the shirt, the individual wears a bright red tight-fitting open waist-length jacket with long sleeves. A series of sixteen buttons runs down the right side of the jacket from the neck to the waist. The lower body is covered by an upper hose and a nether hose. The upper hose is a padded trunk hose reaching down to above the knees. It appears to be paned or pansied with strips of red fabric over a full inner black lining. The lower hose consists of red close-fitting stockings. The black-coloured shoes are ankle height of a flat-soled variety. The individual wears also a black conical hat decorated by gold trimmings and a feather. The dress worn by the gentry-member *fratres hospitalis Sancti Lazari* was very much designed

---

[17] This change in role was initiated in the fourteenth century by the about marked socio-medical changes brought about by the plague pandemics that reduced the prevalence of chronic debilitating disease including leprosy. This changed the ethos of the Order's *raison d'être* so that the leprosy-dedicated hospitaller function changed to a more general one of furnishing hospice and support to the needy ones in the immediate vicinity of the various establishments. This in effect changed the Order into a land-owning establishment using the resources to maintain itself and give solstice to those in need – very much assuming the role of other monastic medicament religious Orders.

according to the fashion of male gentry during the late sixteenth century.[18] There is no sign of the green cross in the illustration.

Le frére hypocrite. 16th century

Head and facial hair

A medieval monk receiving the tonsure (from *St Anselm's De similtudinibus*, 12th century)

Another regulated aspect of the monk's apparel was the hair and facial hair style. During the eight century, male individuals joining a Christian monastic order adopted a very distinctive hairstyle called a tonsure. The origins of this hairstyle are not completely clear, but it may have been adopted to evoke the image of the crown of thorns placed on Jesus's head during his crucifixion. It may also have been adopted to emulate the contemporary practice of shaving the hair of male slaves to indicate the

---

[18] *Le frére hypocrite*. 16th century Illuminated manuscript. San Marino: Huntington Library, ms. HM160, f. 129r. Depicted in R. Hyacinthe, *op. cit.*,, p.170.

concept of 'slaves of Christ'. Whatever its origins, the 'monastic crown' became an integral feature of monastic tradition symbolising religious devotion, the rejection of worldly possessions and confirming the vow of celibacy taken by the monks. Western European monasticism was particularly influenced by St. Benedict of Nursia who founded a monastery at Monte Cassino circa 520 AD and drew up the Rule of St. Benedict which became the basic guide for Western monasticism regulating all aspects of monastic life. While the Rule itself does not specifically mention the need to shave one's head, it does make reference to the 'tonsure' when condemning the Sarabaites who 'In their works they still keep faith with the world, so that their tonsure marks them as liars before God.'[19]

There appeared to have been three types of tonsure known in the early Christian Period. The first form associated with Eastern monasticism consisted of having the whole head shaved. The second form, associated with Western monasticism, involved the shaving of the head leaving a ring of hair around a bald crown. The third form was the Celtic form involved shaving the head from ear to ear. Though the exact shape of the Celtic tonsure is unclear, it may have been semicircular arcing forward from a line between the ears, or assumed a triangular shape with one point at the front of the head going back to a line between the ears.[20] The Roman-style tonsure was adopted as a pre-requisite to receiving the minor and major orders right up to the twentieth century. The 1917 Code of Canon Law decreed that any cleric in minor orders lost his clerical state if he did not resume the tonsure within a month after being warned by his Ordinary. For the monastic clergy, the tonsure area became smaller approximating the size of a priest's host. In 1972, Pope Paul VI in *motu proprio Ministeria quaedam* decreed that the "first tonsure is no longer

[19] Benedict of Nursia, *op. cit.*
[20] Daniel McCarthy. *On the Shape of the Insular Tonsure*. Celtica 2003; 24:pp.140–167.

conferred" effectively abolishing the need for a tonsure to indicate a clerical status.[21]

The three Crusader orders were managed by specific rules and regulations that generally were based on the Benedictine Rule followed by other monastic orders. Membership to these orders was varied and included various levels of status and commitment. These military monastic Order had a varied membership that carried out different functions within the monastery. In the Order of the Temple, the most important members were the warriors who included knights generally coming from a noble family and their *sergents* who supported the knights in battle. Other members of the Order included brothers who served the Order as craftsmen or labourers including those caring for the sick and injured, and priest-brothers who served the spiritual needs of the members. In addition, there were associate members who supported the Order but had not taken full religious vows.[22] As members of a community of a monastic Order, the regular members of the community were obliged to be tonsured. The Latin Rule of the Temple states that 'All brothers, especially the permanent ones, ought to have their hair so tonsured so that normally they can be considered from front or back as regular and ordained. The same rule is to be observed without fail in respect of their beard and whiskers so that no excess or vice of the face may be noted'.[23] The Rule suggests that while the permanent members of the Order were to be tonsured, this was not a formal requirement for

---

[21] Paul VI. *Ministeria Quaedam - Apostolic Letter given Motu Proprio: On first tonsure, minor orders, and the subdiaconate*. Rome: Saint Peter, 15 August 1972. Available at: http://www.ewtn.com/library/PAPALDOC/P6MINORS.HTM

[22] Helen Nicholson. *Knight Templar 1120-1312*. Oxford: Osprey Publ., 2004, pp.10-11

[23] *Latin Rule of 1129. §27 Excessive Hair*. In: Malcolm Barber & Keith Bate (eds). *The Templars*. Manchester: University Press, 2002, p.42

those secular members who joined on a temporary basis. Tombstone effigies belonging to Templar knights generally depict these wearing chainmail coifs covering the head. These knights generally appear to be at least sporting a trimmed moustache.[24]

Sculpture depicting Templar brothers [25]
    Tomb effigy
Raimondo de Bolera[26]

In contrast, the tomb of Don Felipe in the Templar Church of the Commandery of Villasirpa, Palencia depicts four Templar brothers wearing the soft cap and the cape of the Order with the Templar cross insignia on the left. The hairstyle is clearly short being completely contained under the cap. All the brothers are depicted sporting a short-trimmed beard. The presence of a cap does not allow us to conclude on whether these brothers were tonsured. In contrast, the subsequent group of individuals to the right of the Templar group representing a monastic order [? Dominicans] are obviously tonsured and clean shaven. The lay knight holding the capital to the left of the templar groups sports a full crop of hair and is clean shaven. Similarly the late 13th century tomb effigy

---

[24] *Tomb effigy of William Marshall, 1219*. Temple Church, London (U.K.)

[25] Sculpture depicting Templar brothers: *Tomb of Don Felipe, Templar church of Santa Maria la Blanca de Villasirga, at Villacazar de Sirga*. Palencia, Castile (Spain).

[26] *Tomb effigy of preceptor Raimondo de Bolera* at the Church of Sovereto (Italy)

of Raimondo de Bolera shows him to be wearing a cap covering neatly trimmed hair and sporting a trimmed beard and moustache.

The available early 14th century regulations *Dei Regein des Heiligen Orderns S. Lazari* regulated that: 'The gentlemen who are priests, confrères, evangelists and readers, and have had their first consecration, shall appropriately and spiritually have their hair cut and shaved to form a tonsure and are obliged to trim their beards with shear blades for the sake of their office and because of the dignity of the sacrament. But laymen who cannot be consecrated shall wear respectable beards near the mouth together with a moustache. Above the mouth and around it, they shall trim the width of a culm, and their hair shall also be cut appropriately, and, on their heads, they shall wear hoods without pointed ends for protection when it rains or when it is hot.'[27] Fourteenth century tombstone effigies of the masters of the Order suggest a short hairstyle reaching up and covering their ears. The frontal view of the effigies does not allow us to determine whether a tonsure was an integral part of the style. The images show the masters to be clean-shaven.[28]

| Thomas de Sainville 1312 | Jean de Paris 1349 | Jacques de Besnes 1384 |

---

[27] Siegfried von Schlatt, *op. cit.*
[28] Tombeaux de Thomas de Sainville, Jean de Paris et Jacques de Baine, maîtres de l'Ordre de Saint-Lazare de Jérusalem (gravures), *op. cit.*

 The sculptured pedestal serving as the base to a statute of Saint Anthony in the Chapel of Saint-Antoine-de-Grattemont, France show the four knights to have a short hairstyle reaching to the mid-ear level. None show any evidence of a tonsure. All are clean-shaven. The other two medicament brother Lazarites appear to have a similar hairstyle as their knight brothers but appear to include also a Roman-style tonsure. It therefore appears that the members of the Order of Saint Lazarus followed similar regulations in respect to hairstyle as their contemporary military monastic Order of the Temple with the monastic monks being required to show their religious status by wearing a tonsured hairstyle. The other secular members, who sometimes joined on a temporary basis, were not formally required to be tonsured.[29]

Attitudes towards hairstyle within the Hospitaller Military Orders apparently saw a complete change in the subsequent centuries. This change is clearly depicted in 16th century painting showing knights of the Hospitaller Order of St John. The painting by artist Bernardino Pinturicchio of  Alberto Aringhieri in cloak of the Order of the Knights of Jerusalem clearly shows the knight to be sporting a longish non-tonsured hairstyle. Alberto Aringhieri from 1480 served as commander of San Pietro alla Magione,

[29] Pedestal in Chapel of Saint-Antoine-de-Grattemont, *op. cit.*

one of two Sienese possessions of the Order of St. John.[30] A similar change in attitude appears to have taken place also within the Order of St Lazarus.

Conclusion

The members of the Order of Saint Lazarus had strict regulations that influenced all aspects of life within the monastic environment they lived in. In common to the Medieval monastic orders, these regulations determined the dress and general appearance these hospitaller military monks presented to the communities they served. In line with the Augustinian precepts, the general aim was to impress the community not with the apparel worn but with their good moral behaviour.

---

[30] *Alberto Aringhieri kneeling in the costume of a Knight of Jerusalem.* Artist: Bernardino Pinturicchio [lived 1454-1513]. Painting – mixed media on wood panel.

The uniforms of Saint Lazarus during the Baroque and Modern Periods

Abstract

The changing *raison d'être* of the Order of Saint Lazarus throughout the centuries saw the members adopting different clothing styles in accordance to the fashion of the period. The Medieval monkish dress code was gradually replaced with the dress of the novel gentry in accordance to the fashion of the Renaissance Age. The onset of the Baroque Period was to see the adoption of an elaborate flamboyant dress fashion, that was eventually replaced during the Enlightenment Age with a sober rationality towards uniform styles in accordance with the fashion of the time. This has been maintained into the modern period.

Introduction

The seventeenth-century Baroque period was characterised by an elaborate rather eccentric redundancy and excessive abundance of detail, which contrasted to the clear and sober rationality of the preceding Renaissance and the subsequent Enlightenment. The movement is generally believed to have originated in Rome at the beginning of the seventeenth century and spread to France and most of Europe. Generally associated with the artistic movement, the elaborate baroque style was to permeate to various aspects of life including male dress fashion especially that of the nobility and members of the chivalric Orders.

The Order of Saint Lazarus saw its origins in the Kingdom of Jerusalem after the first crusade at the end of the eleventh century. Starting primarily as a Hospitaller Order caring for victims of Hansen's disease [leprosy], the Order eventually assumed a military role participating in various military campaigns against the Islamic forces. The *raison d'être* of the Order changed in the subsequent centuries and, during the Reformation and Counter-Reformation movements 15-16th centuries, the Order was transformed completely from a crusader Hospitaller monkish

Order into a chivalric military one enjoying French royal protection. The changing role of the Order throughout the centuries was reflected by the dress adopted by its members and by the fashion imposed during the baroque age.

The Baroque Age

This was to set the wheels in motion to the adoption of a more flamboyant form of official dress reflecting the change that occurred in western European dress fashion. In the first half of the seventeenth century, the dress fashion changed gradually with the disappearance of the ruff collar to favour broad lace or linen collars. The dress design was generally cut close to the body with tight sleeves and a low, pointed waist. The hose continued to be used. In the second half of the seventeenth century, western European dress fashion gravitated towards a 'dictatorship' of French fashion as determined by the royal court of the powerful Sun King Louis XIV. The body silhouette was transformed to become gradually more softened and broadened with a rise in waistline. Sleeves became fuller and gradually became slashed or paned to show the voluminous sleeves of the shirt or chemise beneath. The hose was replaced by breeches. This period also marked the rise of the periwig as an essential item of men's fashion. During the first decade of the seventeenth century, the Order of Jerusalem was administratively combined with the newly setup Order of Our Lady of Mount Carmel (est. 1608). This required changes in design in the insignia of the members from the use of a green cross to two overlain crosses worn on the front tunic – one green and one amethyst. The dress fashion was also determined by rank being more richly decorated the higher the rank of the individual.

The grand master was the most richly dressed, reflecting his position and authority. A seventeenth century depiction shows him wearing an intricately gold-embroidered white wide-sleeved loose tunic over the standard dress of the time. The underlying shirt was also wide-sleeved edged with wrist lace ruffs. A lace *jabot* was worn tied around the neck. He further wore trunk breeches reaching down to above the knees. The lower hose consists of close-fitting stockings. The shoes were ankle height of a heeled variety. He wore a black hat decorated by gold trimmings and three feathers. His insignia medal was carried as a neck cross.

The chevalier and serving brothers of the Order had similar dress designs wearing a white non-embroidered tunic (the chevalier's tunic was embroidered at the hem) with the green-amethyst cross running all the way down the front. These ranks all wore a body-long voluminous amethyst coloured cape with green lining and depicting the eight-pointed cross of the Order. The grand master's cape was further embroidered with gold and had a marked neck lapel. The novice seemed to be similarly dressed except that the cape was shorter reaching up to the waist. The herald wore a tunic-type overcoat illustrating the arms of the Order on the front. The hussier wore the standard dress *à la française*: a coat, waistcoat, and breeches. Lace jabots were worn tied around the neck while breeches stopped at the knee, with stockings worn underneath and heeled shoes. A skirt-like coat was generally worn open to expose the waistcoats.

Elaborate periwigs in the King Louis XIV style, preferably white, were worn by all members. The ecclesiastic is depicted wearing a dark coloured cassock, or soutane-like garment with a series of buttons down the whole front. This is overlain by a white loose tunic embroidered at the edge. A *mozzetta* or short elbow-length cape with long lapels and depicting the eight-pointed cross of the Order was worn over the shoulder. The insignia medal was carried as a neck cross.

Grand Master *Chevalier* *Serving brother*

Ecclesiastical chevalier *Novice* *Herald*

Hussier
17ᵗʰ century dress of members of the Order.[1]

[1] Pierre Hélyot & Maximilien Bullot. *Histoire des ordres monastiques, religieux et militaires, et des congregations seculieres de l'un et de l'autre sexe, qui ont été établies jusqu'à présent*, Paris: Nicolas Gosselin, 1714, vol. 1, pp. 257-271.

Neoclassical oil-on-canvas painting showing the Comte de Provence wearing the uniform of the Order and pointing to the Statutes of the Order. [2]

The Enlightenment Period

A significant shift in culture which valued reason over authority occurred in France at the beginning of the eighteenth century during the cultural process known as the Enlightenment. New dress fashions introduced now had a greater impact on society, affecting not only royalty and aristocrats, but also the middle and even lower classes. Fashion played a large role in the French Revolution. Patriotically, the revolutionaries characterized themselves by wearing the *tricolor*—red, white, and blue—on items of their clothing. Since the lower working class of the population wore ankle-length trousers, the revolutionaries further

---

[2] Artist: Francois Hubert Drouais [painted: 1770-1775]. Musée national des châteaux de Versailles et de Trianon, Versailles (France).

identified themselves as the *sans-culottes*, or 'without breeches'. This caused knee breeches to become extremely unpopular and even dangerous to wear in France. Anyone caught wearing an extravagant suit was accused of being an aristocrat risking an encounter with Madame Guillotine. The dress fashion influence brought about by the French Revolution initiated a change from the baroque flamboyant dress fashion to the more sombre rather military-style design of men's dress fashion seen during the nineteenth century. The different styles can be contrasted by two portraits of King Louis XVIII, one shown wearing the flamboyant baroque dress emulating his grandfather's late seventeenth-century baroque fashion, and the other wearing the more sombre uniform-like dress adopted in the early nineteenth century. King Louis XVIII served as the last grand master of the Order during the *ancien regime* and as protector until his death in 1824.

Painting of the Comte de Provence as King Louis XVIII wearing the insignia of the Order of Saint Lazarus.[3]

---

[3] Artist: Baron François Gérard [painted: 1823] - Oil on canvas. Musée national des châteaux de Versailles et de Trianon, Versailles (France).

The Modern Period

The rational military-style design for uniforms that came into fashion in the early nineteenth century formed the basis for the uniform design of the early twentieth century. In 1929, a regulation of the administration of the Order specified two outfits – defined as *Tenue de céremonie* and *Tenue hospitaliére*. Each different status within the Order's hierarchy had different minor modifications. In addition, the mantle form was also defined.[4] The first depictions of uniforms in the twentieth century date to the 1930s. This coincides to a period when the Order in France had decided to re-establish the grand magistry linked to the Spanish branch of the Bourbon family.

Advertisement 1934 & Ceremonial Uniform design 1929

These uniforms retain the military-style design together with the adoption of the Church mantle depicting the green eight-pointed cross on

---

[4] *Statuts including Réglement spéciales concerant les insignes et les uniforme de l'Ordre de Saint-Lazare de Jérusalem.* Paris: Journal officiel d'Annonces judiciares et legales, 1929, +8p.

33

the left side. These uniforms were originally advertised for sale from *Jacques Mussier – Taileur Civil et Militaire* of 1 Avenue de la Motte-Piquet, Paris.[5] The official supplier was eventually changed to *Liand – Taileur Civil et Militaire* of 98 Boulevard Sébastopol, Paris. The same supplier was retained right up to at least 1939.[6] The official uniform designs were stipulated within the regulations of the Order. These regulations detailed the various dress protocols including the *Tenue de gala*, the *Tenue de céremonie* and *Tenue hospitaliére*. In addition, the dress of the ecclesiastics and women members was also defined in these regulations.[7]

Advertisement & Uniform design – 1936

[5] Advertisement in: *La Vie Chevaleresque*, 1 January 1934, 2: backpage; 1 July 1934, 6; p.116 [photograph of Chev. B.-J. Gesinus Visser]

[6] Advertisement in: *La Vie Chevaleresque*, April-July 1936, 13: backpage; October 1939, 24/25: backpage.

[7] *La Vie Chevaleresque*, April-July 1936, 13: p.89 [dress regulations], 92; October 1939, 24/25: p.159.

Uniformes

« La couleur de Saint-Lazare, qui est le vert, symbole d'espérance, avec le blanc, couleur qu'on donne à la Vierge, seront le blason et les livrées de l'Ordre qu'on portera dans les costumes, manteaux, armes, cornettes, drapeaux, couvertes et autres équipages de guerre ».

Conformément à cette règle, déjà formulée sous Charles de Nérestang, ces couleurs, avec le noir, couleur basilienne, subsistent dans les uniformes que les membres de l'Ordre portent dans les réunions et les cérémonies.

Actuellement, ils sont classés comme suit : (1)

Une tenue de gala, dont l'essentiel est constitué par un frac de drap vert sombre avec un plastron de drap blanc orné d'une grande croix verte, et bordé d'une broderie en or, une culotte en satin blanc ou un pantalon en drap vert, un bicorne noir à plumes blanches, ou un casque de métal orné d'une plume blanche.

Une tenue de cérémonie, dont l'essentiel est constitué par une tunique de drap blanc à parements verts, une culotte ou un pantalon noir, le bicorne ou le casque ou une casquette de drap.

Une tenue hospitalière, dont l'essentiel est constitué par une tunique ou un veston blanc, un pantalon blanc ou noir ou une culotte noire, le casque ou la casquette.

Ces uniformes comportent selon les circonstances les épaulettes ou les pattes d'épaules, le ceinturon, la bande au pantalon, le sabre ou l'épée avec dragonne, les éperons.

Les boutons sont à la croix verte. Les broderies à trois, deux ou un rang distinguent les grands croix, les commandeurs et les simples chevaliers ou compagnons. Des aiguillettes et des bâtons de commandement sont indicatifs d'offices et de charge. Une cape noire à croix verte accompagne ces costumes, conformément au règlement de François Salviati : « Sur le costume et sur le manteau sera la croix verte à huit pointes ».

Les ornements sont d'or pour les Chevaliers, d'argent pour les Frères d'Armes et les Compagnons.

Il est de tradition que les ecclésiastiques portent sur leur soutane une ceinture verte et des boutons verts, ainsi qu'une mosette avec bordure verte et croix verte. Leur barrette est à bordure verte et pompon vert.

Les Dames peuvent porter le manteau de l'Ordre.

Il n'est pas prévu de costume particulier pour les Croix de Mérite. Une décision particulière du Grand Maître pourrait exceptionnellement autoriser un titulaire à porter l'uniforme de l'Ordre.

Tenue de Gala
G.M. François de Borbón

Ecclesiastical
Canon Jean Tanski

35

Admission Ceremony – 4th April 1937 [8]

New regulations relating to the uniforms relevant to the members of the Order were promulgated in 1968 at a time when the French administration decided to distance itself from its Spanish links deposing the grand master to replace him with H.R.H. Prince Charles Philip of Orleans, Duke of Nemours, Vendôme and Alençon – a member of the pretender family to the French throne. The different dress forms included the *Tenue de gala*, the *Tenue de céremonie, Tenue hospitaliére* and *Tenue d'Eglise*. The regulations also defined the head covering: 'black cocked hat with green and white cockade [with black feathers for knights, white for grand cross]', and church mantle. Two church mantles were defined: one for regular members being made of black cloth with a green eight-pointed cross on the left side, and one for companions made of black cloth with

[8] *La Vie Chevaleresque*, July-September 1937, 17: p.6

an oval fabric badge with a green Latin cross on the left side. Dress codes for ecclesiastics and dames were also defined.[9]

The period under the grand magistry of H.R.H. Prince Charles Philip of Orleans, Duke of Nemours, Vendôme and Alençon saw a move to expand membership to the English-speaking world. This led to specific regulations being promulgated in 1969 to introduce a uniform fashion that was more amiable to the anglophile members while retaining the past continental dress fashion.[10] These decrees identified the uniforms of the Order to consist of:

- *Full Dress*: Rifleman dark green frock coat, white facings, black trousers (or overalls where spurs are worn), cocked hat, and in the case of all commanders of jurisdictions and Grand Officers as above, with feathers. Shoulder badges were defined according to rank. Spurs could be worn according to rank with silver being reserved for commanders and gold for higher ranks.
- *Mess Kit* or tropical kit (undress): a white tunic with green facings and black tie. Otherwise the same as for the Full Dress. The white tunics should be cut in the single military style tunic and not the double-breasted jacket form. This uniform could be worn on all full-dress occasions as an economy measure.
- *Service Dress*: worn by members of the Order and all volunteer organizations of the Order: Dark rifleman green, with black bonnets or berets.

To accommodate past local customs and individuals having older varieties of uniforms, the old uniform could be worn until a new one could be purchased. Mantles or church capes were black lined with the green eight-pointed cross embroidered on the left shoulder, edged with silver for the rank of commanders or below and gold for the rank of knight or above.

---

[9] *Régles, Statuts et Coutumes de l'Ordre de Saint-Lazare de Jérusalem*. Paris: Grand Magistere - MHOSLJ, 1968, +34pp.

[10] GM Decree No. 56/1969, 57/1969, 58/1969, 59/1969. *Constitutional Decrees by 46th Grand Master H.R.H. Prince Charles Philip of Orleans, Duke of Nemours, Vendôme and Alençon*. Netherlands: MHOSLJ, 1969, pp.22-23.

The death of H.R.H. Prince Charles Philip resulted in a return to the grand magistry led by the Spanish Bourbon house. However, the conflict between the French administration and the elected grand master persisted sufficiently to cause a major split within the Order leading to two obediences – the Malta Obedience led by the Spanish grand master, and the French Obedience led by the French leaders. In a move to promote re-unification and accommodate individuals, a comprehensive variety of the previous uniforms became acceptable resulting in three different forms of uniform: the Full Dress [originally the *Tenue de gala*][11], the Dress Uniform [originally the *Tenue de céremonie*], the Evening Winter Uniform [originally the Full Dress], and the Evening Summer Uniform [same as the Full Dress but white coat with green facings and black trousers].[12]

Dress Uniform
Grand Commander Chev. Edward White

Evening Winter Mess Uniform
GM Carlos de Géreda de Borbón

---

[11] Suppliers of the *Tenue de gala* uniform in the 1970s included the costume makers Bermans & Nathans of London.

[12] *The Military and Hospitaller Order of Saint Lazarus of Jerusalem - Uniforms of the Order.* Malta: Grand Chancery – MHOSLJ, undated [c.1980]; GM Decree No.17/1999. See: *The Military and Hospitaller Order of Saint Lazarus of Jerusalem - Constitution, Statutes and General Regulations: Magisterial decree No.17/99.* Malta: GP of Malta-MHOSLJ, 2005.

Following the re-unification of the two major branches in 2006, steps were taken to re-define the formal uniform of the Order bringing it closer in line with a modern gala-style military uniform. [13]

Gala Uniform
GM Francesco de Borbón von Hardenberg

In line with the 2013 regulations:
- The Gala Uniform is the black high-necked jacket and black trousers with green side stripes and green cuffs bearing the appropriate rank insignia. A cap may be worn. Where appropriate, a court sword may be worn.

---

[13] *Regulation No.3 – Wearing of Dress, Decorations, Uniforms, and Insignia. Agreed by the GMC, 8 November 2013*. Grand Magistral Council – MHOSLJ, 2013, +11pp.

- The Mess Dress is the formal dark green uniform with white facings or white with green facings, black trouser with a gold side stripes and epaulettes bearing the appropriate rank insignia. It is worn with a black bow tie and black waistcoat.
- The Scottish Dress, allowed for Scottish members or those with Scottish heritage, is an appropriate Scottish jacket and accoutrements with kilt or trews, and black or white tie as appropriate. A Scottish basket-hilted broadsword and/or a Balmoral or Glengarry bonnet may be worn where appropriate.
- Female members wear a black or dark-coloured dress (long for formal and evening wear, shorter for day wear), and for wear and church services, mantilla and comb or equivalent head covering. The appropriate uniform may also be worn with a plain black skirt substituting the trousers in desired.
- Informal dress involves the use of a traditional blazer-style black or dark jacket with gold Saint Lazarus buttons and the full achievement of the plain white arms of the Order of Saint Lazarus embroidered on the front pocket.
- The Church Cape or Mantle is a black cape reaching to about 15 cm above the ground with a dark-green collar lined with emerald green silk-like material. A green gold-bordered eight=pointed cross of about 30 cm is embroidered on the left breast. Neck fastening is by a gold chain from two clasps, either lion-faced or showing the Saint Lazarus cross.

The female dress of the Order

Abstract

At its origins, the Order of Saint Lazarus incorporated a female element originally serving the female sick but eventually adopting a more spiritual charisma. These Lazarite nuns adopted the dress usually worn by other female monastic orders, possibly incorporating the green cross as part of their identity insignia. These female Lazarite establishments were apparently disbanded and incorporated within other monastic orders during the 15-16th centuries. A female component within the Order f Saint Lazarus was only re-established in the early decades of the twentieth century.

Introduction

The Order of Saint Lazarus, in common with the other Hospitaller orders, had a female element to its overall organization looking to assist female victims of leprosy. With the waning of the Order's Hospitaller role during the fifteenth century and the increasing movement towards assuming a military and honorific role, the female element disappeared from the Order's organization, only to be re-assumed in the modern restructuring that occurred during the twentieth century.[1]

The Medieval Period

The Order of Saint Lazarus during the medieval period had a number of female-based establishments in the Outremer, France, and Central Europe. These generally had a monastic life existence generally initially following a Benedictine charisma that was changed in the mid-13th century to an Augustinian one.

---

[1] Charles Savona-Ventura. *Wine, Women & Song: Female members of the Order*. Acta Historiae Sancti Lazari Ordinis, 2019, 3: pp.181-194.

The religious habit of Benedictine or Augustinian nuns basically consists of a loose tunic pleated at the neck and draping to the ground. It was made originally from undyed wool [i.e. white or grey] habits, but with time black became the prevailing colour. The habit was tied around the waist with a cincture of cloth or leather belt. The habit contains two sets of sleeves, the larger of which can be worn folded up for work or folded down for ceremonial occasions or whenever entering a chapel. The scapular is a symbolic apron hanging from both front and back worn over the tunic. The coif is the headpiece made of a white cotton cap secured by a bandeau and a white wimple or guimpe of starched linen to cover the cheeks and neck. A veil could also be pinned over the coif head coverings. Simple functional black shoes were the usual footwear. A variety of styles of aprons could be worn over the habit to protect it during work activities.

Benedictine Nun [2]

Augustinian Nun

[2] Gasquet. English Monastic Life. London: Metheun & Co., 1904, p.216

It is not clear whether the sisters of the Order of Saint Lazarus were obliged to wear the green cross insignia on their habits as their male counterparts. The statutes do not however distinguish between male and female members of the Order, and hence it can be assumed that the nuns wore the green Crusader Cross. The sisters in the Convents of Gfenn and Seedorf were in 1418 definitely obliged to 'go out in their habit and serve God as far as they can', thus confirming the use of a monastic habit. There is no mention of an incorporated green cross.[3]

The only identified potential Medieval depiction of a Lazarite nun is a tomb effigy from the Notre Dame de

Tomb effigy in Notre Dame de Tyre Nunnery, Nicosia

Tyre Nunnery in Nicosia, Cyprus [established as a nunnery under Benedictine Rule in 1310 as a result of a legacy left to the *Infirmis Sancti Lazari*]. However, the cut of the dress worn by the effigy suggests the individual to be a high society individual rather than a member of a monastic order. There is no depiction of the Crusader cross on the left

[3] Siegfried von Schlatt. *Ordinis equitum Sancti Lazari Hierosolymitani RRegulae vel Statuta Gevenn Seedorfque Domibus anno MCDXVIII promulgata*. Ms. Seedorf Monastery. Ms. 1314/31. Transcribed and translated by Prof. H.C. Vella in: Charles Savona-Ventura [editor]. *Die Regül deß Heiligen Ordens S. Lazari 1314/1321 zu 1418 - The Rules of the Holy Order of S. Lazarus 1314/1321 to 1418*. Lulu Ltd., U.S.A., 2020.

breast of the effigy. [4] The Lazarite sisters would however have probably emulated their counterpart sisters in the Order of Saint John who are believed to have worn the cross insignia.

Portrait of a nun of the Order of Saint John [5]

The Modern Period

The changing roles linked with the Order of Saint Lazarus during the 16th century led to an exclusive role for male members. A sisterhood element became irrelevant, and most Lazarite nunneries were closed down or assimilated with formal female monastic orders. A female membership was again re-constituted in the early part of the twentieth century.[6] The 1929 regulations state: *15° Les dames n'ont pas d'iniforme*

---

[4] Michel Willis. Notre Dame de Tyre, more recently the Armenian Church, medieval tomb slab, photograph taken 1973. Zenodo, 2017, http://doi.org/10.5281/zenodo.267982

[5] Portrait of St Ubaldesca – sister of the Order of Saint John. Artist unknown; Oil on canvas 18th century. Museum of the Order of St John, London, LDOSJ:1730

[6] C. Savona-Ventura, *op. cit.*

particulier. Mais sur les directives du Grand Prévôt, maître general des cérémonies, le ceremoniaire de chaque Grand Prieuré ou Commandeerie peut indiquer la tenue qu'elles devront avoir, pour pouvoir, dan s les ceremonies de l'Ordre, avoir droit à des places spéciales, il peut, notamment, prescrire le port d'une mantilla. [7]

The mantle with the green eight-pointed cross on the left chest remained the sole official apparel for the dames of the Order, worn over suitable attire for the occasion. This generally required a dark coloured dress. In the 1980s, dress regulation for female members were defined as a plain black velvet mantle lined in green silk, preferably over a long black dress with full sleeves, with a black mantilla and comb.[8] The 2016 revision of the dress regulations state that: 'Ladies should wear a black or dark-coloured dress (long for formal and evening wear, shorter for day wear), and a formal wear and church services, mantilla and comb (where capes will be worn, ladies wear a half-mantilla) or an equivalent head-covering may be appropriate. In general, ladies should wear decorations using the same pattern as for men at the same function, but with only one decoration on a bow, if they are not in uniform. Ladies who hold office in the Order may wear the appropriate uniform of the Order but may substitute a plain black skirt for trousers if they so choose. [9]

---

[7] *Statuts including Réglement spéciales concerant les insignes et les uniforme de l'Ordre de Saint-Lazare de Jérusalem.* Paris: Journal officiel d'Annonces judiciares et legales, 1929, +8p.

[8] *The Military and Hospitaller Order of Saint Lazarus of Jerusalem - Uniforms of the Order.* Malta: Grand Chancery – MHOSLJ, undated [c.1980]; GM Decree No.17/1999. See: *The Military and Hospitaller Order of Saint Lazarus of Jerusalem - Constitution, Statutes and General Regulations: Magisterial decree No.17/99.* Malta: GP of Malta-MHOSLJ, 2005.

[9] *Regulation No.3 – Wearing of Dress, Decorations, Uniforms, and Insignia. Agreed by the GMC, 18 November 2016.* Grand Magistral Council – MHOSLJ, 2016, +25pp.

1970s Group photograph including dame members of the Order

2018 Group photograph including female members of the Order

The eight-pointed breast cross

Abstract

The cross insignia of the Crusader Orders is believed to have originated from the practice of distributing crosses to individuals undertaking a crusade in the Outremer. These simple cloth crosses were to be sewn onto the cloak. Their form gradually changed from a simple form to the eight-pointed triangular cross.

Introduction

Individuals undertaking a crusade in the Outremer were given a cloth cross to be sewn on the cloak or mantle. This cross was assumed to have miraculous and protective properties. The Crusader Orders all assumed the standard crusader cross insignia differentiating themselves by different coloured crosses – red for the Templar knights, white for the Hospitallers, green for the Lazarites, and black for the Teutonic knights.

Pope Urban II distributing crusader crosses

The form of the cross insignia evolved over time to assume an eight-pointed triangular edged form for two of the Crusader orders – the Hospitallers of St John the Baptist and the Order of St Lazarus. It is difficult to correctly trace the origins of the use of the triangularly armed eight-pointed cross in heraldry. Controversy exists regarding the actual original form of the eight-pointed cross of the Order promulgated by the mythological grandiose association of the cross with the eight beatitudes invented by the Order's historians. The date for this modification in the context of the Order of St John is difficult to identify from historical sources. One must delve into the archaeological artefacts relevant to the Order to identify the development of the cross insignia. An 11th century association has also been made with the design found on coins minted in the southern Italy coastal town of Amalfi. The Amalfi cross was itself commonly incorporated in many of the Crusader coins minted in the Outremer.[1] The Amalfi and Outremer cross depicted on the 12th century coins clearly represents a *cross formeé*.

Amalfi-minted coin, 1194   **Outremer-minted coin, Baldwin III c.1143**

The Armenian and Bolnisi-type crosses are clearly evident incised on the Crusader Period walls as one descends to St. Helen's Chapel in the Holy Sepulchre in Jerusalem.

---

[1] R. Weetch. *Crusader coins in Antioch*. Bearers of the Cross: Material Religion in the Crusading World, 1095-c1300. Birminghan (U.K.): University of Birmingham, 2016, https://www.bearersofthecross.org.uk/interpreting-the-collections/crusader-coins-museum-order-st-john/antioch/

Crusader Period incised crosses: Holy Sepulchre, Jerusalem

The Cross of the Order of St. John of Jerusalem

The 12th century seal of the second master of the Order of St John in Jerusalem, Raymond de Puy, depicts the Patriarchal cross with two crossbars. The general design of the seal featured, on the obverse, the Master kneeling in prayer before the patriarchal cross. The Master is not depicted carrying any particular insignia. The reverse of the seal depicted a dead body lying before a tabernacle. The surrounding legend seems to identify the institution as HOSPITALIS IHERVSALEM. The design was retained right through the subsequent decades with the eventual incorporation of the Armenian cross on a shaft being depicted at the head of the dead body. The seal of Garin de Montaigu (1207-1228) does depict an eight-pointed cross incorporated within the text on the obverse and reverse side. On close inspection, the form of the cross appears to be a Bolnisi-type cross. [2]

The statutes of the Order of St John as promulgated by Raymond du Puy (1120-1160) require "all the brothers of the hospital be obliged to wear a black robe or mantle with a white cross." These were further modified by master Nicolas de Lorgue (1277-1285) stating that "We enact likewise, that in the exercise of arms they wear over their clothes a red military cloak, with the white cross strait." There was no specific mention

---

[2] B. Pachard. *Seals of the Grand Masters*. London (U.K.): Museum of the Order of St John, 2019, http://museumstjohn.org.uk/seals-of-the-grand-masters/

of an eight-pointed cross. The "white cross with eight points" was only mentioned in the 1489 revision of the Statutes of the Order of St John. [3]

Seal of Raymond de Puy [1120-1160]   **Seal of Garin de Montaigu [1207-1228]**

Together with all the Crusader forces, the Order of St John was expelled from Acre in 1291. The turmoil caused by the displacement prompted the Order to invade Rhodes in 1310 establishing the island into an independent sovereign state. This allowed the Order of St John to start minting its own currency. The design of the early minted currency was similar to the earlier seals showing the master praying before the Patriarchal cross. However, the detail further shows the master to be carrying the cross insignia on the left shoulder. The cross form appears to be a Bolnisi-type cross. This design was retained right through the 15th century.

Hélion de Villeneuve   *Philibert de Naillac*   *Jacques de Milly*
1319-1346   *1396-1421*   *1454-1461*
                         Rhodian coins

[3] *The Old and New Statutes of the Order of St John of Jerusalem*. In: R. de Vertot. The History of the Knights of Malta. London (U.K.): G. Strahan, 1728, vol.2, p.11.

16th century tomb effigy of knight, Rhodes ©CSV

Tombstone of Pierre de Corneillan, Musée de Cluny, Paris.

The depiction of the cross over the left shoulder is also evident in tombstones effigies dating from the Rhodian period such as that of grand master Pierre de Corneillan (1353-1355). The cross depicted on the tombstone appears to resemble an elongated Bolnisi-type cross. This format was apparently retained through the 15th century. The 1489 Statutes of the Order of St John required the knights to wear "the white cross with eight points".[4] This requirement does not however clearly define the type of eight-pointed cross used and could refer to any format. By the early 16th century, the cross depicted on the cloak appears to have assumed a relatively triangular format similar to the modern form. A tomb effigy dated to the 16th century in the Archaeological Museum housed in the old Hospital of the Order in Rhodes depicts a knight of the Order with an eight-pointed cross on the mantle. While the cross arms are not exactly straight edged, the curvature may have been purposefully carved to reflect a three-dimensional depiction of the cloak. This depiction on the cloak conforms to the modern-style form used by the Order of Saint John of Malta. The knights were expelled from Rhodes in 1522.

The development of the cross shape from an Armenian-type to a Bolnisi-type cross is shown in a quadrangular fountain in Argyrocastrou Square, in the old city of Rhodes. The fountain is decorated on its four sides by two cross forms. The first form carved on two sides of the fountain depicts an Armenian-style cross; the second form depicts a Bolnisi-type cross.

Fountain in Argyrocastrou Square, Rhodes showing Armenian and Bolnisi Crosses

[4] *Stabilimenta Rhodiorum militum: die Statuten des Johanniterordens von 1489/93*. In: Jyri Hasecker & Jürgen Sarnowsky [eds.]. *Nova mediaevalia*. V&R Unipress, 2007, vol. 1.

| Greek Cross | Armenian Cross | Bolnisi Cross | "Maltese" Cross |

The archaeological evidence therefore suggests that the cross of the Order of Saint John evolved from the Armenian-type cross used during in the Outremer, being modified into the curved-edged Bolnisi-type cross in during the Rhodian Period to finally assuming the straight-edged triangular eight-pointed cross. The knights were expelled from Rhodes in 1522.[5] Clear depictions of the straight-edged triangular eight-pointed so-called "Maltese" cross are evident on coins minted during the 16th century in Malta. The coins minted in Malta also confirm that the knights wore their cross insignia on the mantle and/or armour.

Maltese coin, Claude de la Sengle
1553-57

Maltese coin, Jean de la Vallette
1557-1568

Philippe de Villiers de L'Isle-Adam
1464-1534

António Manoel de Vilhena
1663-1736

---

[5] M. Foster. *History of the Maltese Cross as used by the Order of St John of Jerusalem.* http://www.lishfd.org/History/history_of_the_maltese_cross.htm, 2004.

The specific Maltese Cross logo of the Sovereign Military Order of Malta is today clearly defined by Article 6 of the Constitutional Charter of the SMOM as being a "white eight-pointed cross (cross of Malta) on a red field".[6] In addition, the members of the SMOM also use the white eight-pointed cross on black insignia for their capes and medals.

The Cross of the Order of Saint Lazarus of Jerusalem

A similar developmental history can be traced in respect to the Order of St Lazarus of Jerusalem. Like the Order of St John, the knights of the Order of St Lazarus identified themselves by wearing a green Greek Cross on a white surcoat [similar to the red Greek Cross on a white surcoat of the Templar knights]. This developed in subsequent centuries into a green Greek Cross *pattée* on a white or black mantle. The fourteenth-century statutes of the Order of St Lazarus prescribed the wearing of a square [i.e. Greek] green cross insignia sewn onto the front of the habit, left side of the mantle and the harness. When they went to war, their helmet, shield and all pieces of armour were to be distinctly marked with a cross of the same shape and colour.[7] The use of the green cross was by the 1419 extended to all the members of the Order including tenants, domestics and commandery servants. In the mid-16th century, political developments in France required the adoption of the practice of appointing members of the Order of St John as grand masters of the Order of St Lazarus. One of these grand masters, François de Salviati in the Chapter General held in 1578 undertook to formally modify the insignia of the Order of St Lazarus. The previous Greek Cross pattern for members of the Order of St Lazarus was now modified into 'an eight-pointed cross vert'. Individuals who held joint membership in the Order of St Lazarus

---

[6] *Constitutional Charter of the Sovereign Military Hospitaller Order of St John of Jerusalem of Rhodes and of Malta promulgated 27 June 1961 and revised by the Extraordinary Chapter General 28-30 April 1997*. Rome, 1998.

[7] Siegfried von Schlatt. (1314/31). *Dei Regein des Heiligen Orderns S. Lazari*. Ms. Seedorf Monastery. Transcribed and translated in: Charles Savona-Ventura [editor]. *Die Regül deß Heiligen Ordens S. Lazari 1314/1321 zu 1418 - The Rules of the Holy Order of S. Lazarus 1314/1321 to 1418*. Lulu Ltd., U.S.A., 2020.

and of St John were to superimpose the two eight-pointed crosses resulting in 'an eight-pointed cross vert with an argent bordure'.[8]

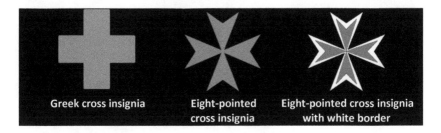

Greek cross insignia | Eight-pointed cross insignia | Eight-pointed cross insignia with white border

The eight-pointed triangular-armed cross sown on the mantle was modified in the beginning of the 17th century when the Crusader Order of Saint Lazarus was amalgamated by Henri IV with the newly established Order of Our Lady of mount Carmel [established 1608]. The regulations dates 1649 state that : *'Nul que les susdits Grand Maistre, primats & Haut Officers, pourra porter la Croix sue le manteaux ordinaire toute en birderie d'or & d'argent, au blazon de l'Ordre. Mais les autre la porteront d'estosse de soye, orlée d'argent & la Vierge rayonnée d'or.'* The Cross of the Order was described as: *'d'or, enuiron de trois poulces de diameter, sa figure doit ester octogone, c'est à dire à 8 pointes, pommettées d'or, & la Croix flanquée de 4 fleure de lys d'or. La Croix sera double, la premiere qui est la plus grande, est celle de Notre Dame à l'email tanné amaranthe. La 2, est la plus petite, chargeé sur l'autre, & cest celle de Saint Lazare, à l'email verd.'* The cross further carried two medals, one showing the image of Our Lady of Mount Carmel; the other that of Resurrection of St Lazarus.[9] This cross was to be worn as a neck decoration.

---

[8] J.J. Algrant y Canete & de J. Beaugourdon. *Armorial de l'Ordre Militaire et Hospitalier de Saint Lazare de Jerusalem – Armoral de la Orden Militar y Hospitalaria de San Lazaro de Jerusalén – Armorial of the Military and Hospitaller Order of Saint Lazarus of Jerusalem* (p.cccclvi). Holland: H.A. van den Akker, 1980.

[9] *Memoires, Regles et Statuts, Ceremonies et Privileges des Ordres Militaires de Notre Dame du Mont Carmel et de S. Lazare de Jerusalem.* Lyon: Antoine Cellier, 1649, pp.99-101

Philibert de Nerestang
wearing the eight-pointed
insignia cross - 1608

17th century neck cross of the Orders of Our Lady of
Mount Carmel and of Saint Lazarus of Jerusalem
[reverse & obverse sides]

The breast cross was again introduced after the re-organization that was carried out in 1778 that separated the two Orders. These new regulations decreed that the mark of the profession for knights of the irst classe was: '*une croix brodée sur le côté gauche du l'habit, en paillons d'or vert, entourée de paillettes d'or, surmontée au milieu d'une croix d'argent, avec le chiffre de Saint-Lazare en or sur le blanche d'en haut, et celui de la Santé Vierge sur la branche d'en bas, et au milieu, cette légende en lettres d'or, Atavis et Armis.*' This was worn in addition to a neck cross.[10] The breast cross insignia continued to be used right through the early decades of the nineteenth century, being depicted in portraits as adorning the uniforms of several individuals.

---

[10] *Reglement du comte de Provence du 3 decembre 1778*. Transcribed in: Garden de Saint-Ange. *Code des ordres de chevalierie du royaume, ouvrage contenant les statuts fondamentaux des ordres, les lois, ordonnances*. France, 1819, pp.412-423 [1978 Edition: Guy Tredaniel, France, pp.368-447]

King Louis XVIII (1755-1824) wearing the breast green eight-pointed cross in portrait dated 1823

Breast eight-pointed cross 18-19th century

Count Peter Ludwig von der Pahlen (1745-1826) Military Governor of St. Petersburg, wearing neck & breast cross

Marquis Marc Marie de Bombelles (1744–1822) French diplomat and ecclesiastic, wearing neck & breast cross

The history of the Order of Saint Lazarus during the latter half of the 19th century is shrouded in mystery as a result of deficient documentation but it appears that the Order was taken over by Pope Pius IX to use as an award for the pontifical zouaves who supported his cause during the *Risorgimento* unification movement in Italy. Following the fall of Rome in 1872, the zouaves were disbanded but re-organized themselves in the

Militia di Gesu pledged to continue supporting the Holy See against threats.[11] The first documented breast star produce during this period was manufactured by the Italian jewellers CRAVANZOLA GUARDINO produced during the 1871-1913 period. The design of the breast star is based on the 18th century design of the neck cross of the French Order of St Lazarus and includes the green-edged-white eight-pointed cross with the points ending in golden orbs depicting the beatitudes. Four fleur-des-lys are placed between the arms of the cross reflecting the past links with the French royal house even though the Order had lost the protection of the French royal house in 1831. The whole is mounted on an eight-pointed star; while a plaque encircled by the motto ATAVIS ET ARMIS depicting the raising of St Lazarus is mounted in front. The breast star is clearly marked on the back with the imprint D. CRAVANZOLA SUCC. FLLI BORANI. ROMA.[12]

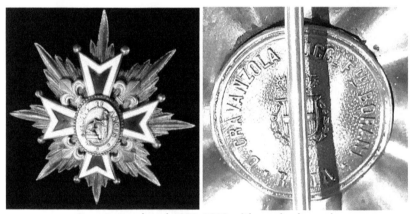

Breast star dated 1871-1913 with marker's mark

[11] Charles Savona-Ventura. The fons honorum of the Order of Saint Lazarus: 1800-1910. *Acta Historiae Sancti Lazari Ordinis*, 2019, 3:65-90. This breast star was originally brought to the attention of the author by H.E. Chev the Count d'Évora.
[12] Vide: https://www.emedals.com/italy-kingdom-an-order-of-st-maurice-lazarus-in-gold-grand-cross-by-d-cravanzola-c-1900;
https://www.astebolaffi.it/it/lot/380/15/detail;

The link with the French royal house was definitely broken with the subsequent breast cross design with the exclusion of the fleur de lys. The 1910 published statutes define the insignia of the re-organized Order as: *La Croix des Chevaliers Hospitaliers forme quatre branches égales de sinople bordées d'or, qui s'épanouissent en huit pointes en signe des Béatitudes auxquelles ils devent aspirer. Elle porte à l'avers l'omage de Saint Lazare issant du tombeau entourée de la devise ATAVIS ET ARMIS et au revers l'image de la B.V.M. Cette Croix, soutenue par une double chaine d'or, n'est point surmontée d'une couronne souveraine car la mission des Chevaliers s'exerce spécialement aux Lieux Saints où N.S.J.-C. n'a porté au'une couronne d'épines.*[13] Various forms of gilded and enamelled breast stars and neck cross insignia were produced during the period 1902-1937 with a green-edged with white cross used for members of the aristocracy, and a totally green cross for non-aristocratic members.[14]

Knight [gold gilded]

Commander [silver]

**Breast star for aristocratic members
1902-1937**

**Breast star for non-aristocratic
members 1902-1937**

---

[13] de Jandriac. *Les chevaliers Hospitaliers de Saint Lazare de Jerusalem et de Notre Dame de la Merci.* Rivista Araldica, November 1913, XI(11): pp.679-683.

[14] Dorotheum Auctions. Palais Dorotheum, Dorotheergasse 17, 1010 Vienna (Austria). Expert: Dr. Georg Ludwigstorff. Vide: https://www.dorotheum.com/de/l/1347256/; https://www.dorotheum.com/de/l/1347250/; https://www.dorotheum.com/de/l/1347253/ https://www.dorotheum.com/de/l/1347244/; https://www.dorotheum.com/de/l/1347247/

| Knight's neck cross for non-aristocratic members 1902-1937 | Dame neck cross for non-aristocratic members 1902-1937 |

The first 20th century depiction of the insignia worn by the members of the Order of St Lazarus dates to 1934. The breast star is similar in shape to the one produced by the Borani Brothers earlier but differs in that the four fleur-des-lys between the four arms of the green edged with white eight-pointed cross are replaced by interlaced SL [depicted as a three-branched design]. Individuals awarded the grand cross of merit wore a *'plaque de même forme, dont les rayons sont argents.'*[15] The overall design was generally very standard, however the SL design very much dependant on the jewellers commissioned to produce the insignia. Another 1930 design from French jewellers shows a significantly different SL design.[16]

Breast stars dated to the mid-1930s

---

[15] Charles Otzenberger-Detaille. *Les insignes de l'Ordre de saint-Lazare de Jérusalem*. La Vie Chevaleresque, 1934, 6:pp.110-111.

[16] The jewellers responsible for these French-produced insignia are not identified.

The overall design since, as exemplified by the breast stars has remained the same with minor alterations being made depending on the jewellers and country of origin.[17]

| probably by Cejalvo, Madrid (1954-1972)[18] | Grand Priory of Bohemia (undated) |

The development of schismatic groups gave rise to even more varieties in the form of the breast star insignia especially in distinguishing between the categories of membership to the Order and of membership to the Order of Merit. Silver gilding, in lieu of gold gilding, was also used to distinguish between Knight/Dame and Commander breast stars.[19] The Orleans Obedience have since re-adopted the interlacing fleur de lys [20] since they have been placed under the protection of the Pretender to the French Crown Henri d'Orleans [died 21 January 2019 succeeded by his son Jean d'Orleans].[21]

[17] Dorotheum Auctions. *op. cit.* Vide: https://www.dorotheum.com/de/l/1347241/; https://www.dorotheum.com/de/l/1347202/

[18] The establishment *Joyeros Artesanos Cejalvo S L* of Madrid was founded in 1860. An identical design ?post-WWII gold-plated breast star was produced by the establishment *C. Jordana* sited at Principe 7, Madrid. Sale offer on eBay dated 3rd November 2020.

[19] Stuart G. Morris. *The Insignia and decorations of the military and Hospitaller Order of Saint Lazarus of Jerusalem*. Scotland; MHOSLJ, 1986.

[20] Dorotheum Auctions. *op. cit.* Vide: https://www.dorotheum.com/de/l/1347211/; https://www.dorotheum.com/de/l/1347208/

[21] The legitimacy of Jean d'Orleans is contested by two other pretenders: Louis de Bourbon, Duke of Anjou (a direct descendant of Louis XIV), and Jean-Christophe Napoléon (a descendant of Emperor Napoléon III).

GCLJ/KCLJ/DCLJ
probably by Cejalvo, Madrid (1972)

CLJ
Toye, Henning & Spencer London (1972)[22]

DMLJ [gold plated]

CMLJ [silver plated]

GCMLJ/KMLJ
Toye, Henning & Spencer London (2019)

DMLJ & CMLJ
Toye, Henning & Spencer London (1972)

Malta Obedience Order of Merit Breast stars

GCLJ/KCLJ/DCLJ de Justice
by Bacqueville, Paris (1972)[23]

GCLJ/KCLJ/DCLJ de Merite
by Bacqueville, Paris (1972-2004)

---

[22] *Toye, Kenning & Spencer* of London craftsmen have created identity products for civil and military markets since 1685.

[23] *Maision Bacqueville* of Paris was established in 1790.

GCMLJ/KMLJ/DMLJ d'Emerite d'Honneur
by Bacqueville, Paris
Paris Obedience Breast stars

(post-2004)   by Friedrich Orth, Vienna (post-2004)

Orleans Obedience Breast stars

The Order's magazine *La Vie Chevaleresque* during 1934 repeatedly carried an advertisement for *Maison L. Bonnesoeur* of Paris. This establishment was founded in 1886 and produced engravings on metal for seals, stamps, puncher presses, etc. supplying administrations, Ministries. Consulates, Chivalric Orders, etc. There is however no record of this establishment producing medals for the Order of Saint Lazarus. Another engraver *Maison L. Spilman* of Paris – appears in later 1938 editions of the magazine. There is however no record of these establishments ever producing medals or breast stars for the Order of Saint Lazarus. [24]

---

[24] *La Vie Chevaleresque*. 1934, 4:backpage; 1938, 21-22:backpage

Advertisements for *Graveur* establishments
in *La Vie Chevaleresque* 1934/1938

The history of heraldry within the Order

Abstract

Heraldry is an integral facet of a Chivalric Order which is charactyerised by definite arms and further requires its members to register any heraldic arms they may possess. The developmental history of heraldry within the Order of Saint Lazarus is here reviewed/

Introduction

Heraldry found a general utilitarian application in Western Europe from the second quarter of the 12th century being regularly used on armour in warfare and on seals in peacetime. In addition, in the later medieval period, it became associated with the concept of gentility. Heraldic emblems, worn on the shield and surcoat served to distinguish a man in armour, while badges distinguished his followers. The emblems were also carried into the battlefield on standards to serve as rallying points during the conflict. This use of heraldry found a further role for identifying individuals in the form of seals accompanying important documents. This led to heraldic arms being adopted by municipalities, churches, and colleges. The establishment of the Crusader Orders as a fighting force in the Outremer further led to the adoption of heraldic insignia representing the organization, sometimes combined with the coat-of-arms of the individual. A study of the heraldry related to the Crusader Orders, including that of the Order of Saint Lazarus, thus involves two aspects: (1) the development of the specific heraldic insignia of the organization, and (2) the incorporation of that organizational insignia within the personal coat-of-arms of the individual members. The Baroque and later Rococo periods, characterized by exaggerated detail to produce exuberance and grandeur in the arts, affected also the way the iconographic representations of heraldry were presented to amply emphasise the importance of the individual or organization. This period saw the added introduction of the use of helms (incorporating the crest, torses or coronets, and mantling) above the shield, supporters, mottoes, and mantles.

Heraldic insignia of the Crusader Orders

At the end of the 11th century, Pope Urban II issued a general call to the faithful encouraging them to assemble a military force with the aim of liberating the Holy Land from the forces of evil. Those that responded were given cloth badges depicting the Crusader Cross to wear on their left side of their robe to confirm the individual to be a Soldier of Christ, a Crusader.[25] The Crusader Orders in the Outremer adopted different coloured crosses as identity or armorial badges. The Order of St. Lazarus adopted the green cross while the other military orders adopted different coloured crosses. The earliest heraldic depiction of the Order of Saint Lazarus appears on a sculptured pedestal serving as the base to a statute of Saint Anthony in the Chapel of Saint-Antoine-de-Grattemont, France dated to 1480. This has been painted to depict a green Latin cross placed centrally of a black shield. [26]

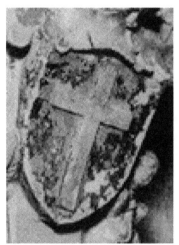

15th century heraldic arms of the Order of Saint Lazarus

---

[25] St. Gallen, Stiftsbibliothek, Cod. Sang. 658, p.25 – (1) Robertus Monachus, History of the first Crusade (illustrated); (2) Ottokar von Steiermark, rhymed chronicle of Austria: the fall of Akkon (https://www.e-codices.ch/en/list/one/csg/0658)

[26] Pedestal in Chapel of Saint-Antoine-de-Grattemont, France. Depicted in Raphael Hyacinthe. L'Ordre de Sant-Lazare de Jerusalem au Moyen Age. Millau: Conservatoire Larzac Templier et Hospitalier, 2003, pp.134-135.

The original reason as to why the colour green was chosen to represent the Order of Saint Lazarus can only be left to conjecture. The first documented mention of the origins of the green cross insignia for the Order dates to the statutes written by Siegfried von Schlatt in 1314/21: 'The origin of the holy green cross which started in the Old Testament and was fulfilled in the New Testament is as follows: it epitomizes the cross of our Lord Jesus Christ, which was made of four cut timbers, and later was used to represent the four principal Orders of crusaders. The first timber was from a cypress, the second from a palm, the third from a cedar and the fourth from an olive tree. If the palm is now evergreen and tall, and has pointed leaves and produces sweet fruits, just as the soul speaks in songs – I want to go to the palm tree and touch its fruit – so in the same way the palm seems to best epitomize the symbol of the green cross of this Holy Order, whose links shall be green and grow on good life. Because everything that is green in nature grows and bears fruit. But the palm tree is high above itself and thus also the soul of the spiritual person shall rise high above itself and shall acquire the Heavenly Kingdom with divine contemplation. But the tree has pointed leaves which means that the human being shall willingly shoulder rigorous hardships because of the crucified Christ, whose body has become strong on the Holy Cross when death struggled with him and when the death of Jesus Christ destroyed eternal death thus giving us back our life through his resurrection.'[27]

The Baroque age saw a change in the heraldic depiction of the green eight-pointed cross insignia in line with the artistic development of the period. The arms of the Order were depicted on a commemorative medallion minted in 1700 and 1757 during the grand masterships of Philippe de Courcillon and Louis de France de Berry [eventually King Louis XVI]. These arms show the Greek cross within a central oval shield superimposed over the eight-pointed cross and encircled by the neck

---

[27] Siegfried von Schlatt. *Dei Regein des Heiligen Orderns S. Lazari. Ms. Seedorf Monastery. Ms. 1314/21*. Transcribed and translated in: Charles Savona-Ventura. *Die Regül deß Heiligen Ordens S. Lazari 1314/1321 zu 1418 - The Rules of the Holy Order of S. Lazarus 1314/1321 to 1418*. U.S.A.: Lulu Ltd, 2020, p.100.

collars of the Order of St Lazarus and the Order of Our Lady of Mount Carmel, the latter surmounted by the Eastern crown.

*Arms of the Order of St Lazarus on commemorative medallions
dated 1700 & 1757*

The Baroque age further saw a change from the simple green Latin cross on a black shield depicted in the 15th century heraldry to a more flamboyant form drawn in the 18th century manuscript *Armorial général* held by the *Bibliothèque nationale de France* in Paris. The same manuscript further depicts the post-1608 heraldic arms of the united Orders of St Lazarus [OSL] and Our Lady of Mount Carmel [OLMC] combining the heraldic green of the Order of St Lazarus with the heraldic amethyst of the Order of Our Lady of Mount Carmel. In a very graphic heraldic fashion, these depictions incorporate the individuals and institutions that had a formal and legal relationship with the two Orders.[28]

---

[28] Vincent Thomassin. *Armorial général des Ordres royaux, militaires et hospitaliers de N.-D. du Mont-Carmel et de Saint-Lazare de Jérusalem, recherché et recueilly par frère Claude Dorat de Chameulles,... présenté à MM. les Chanoines réguliers de l'abbaye royale de Saint-Victor de Paris par M. Vincent Thomassin, avocat au parlement, juge-garde armorial desdits Ordres, en 1753*. Bibliothèque nationale de France, Département des manuscrits, Français 23135, 96 fols.

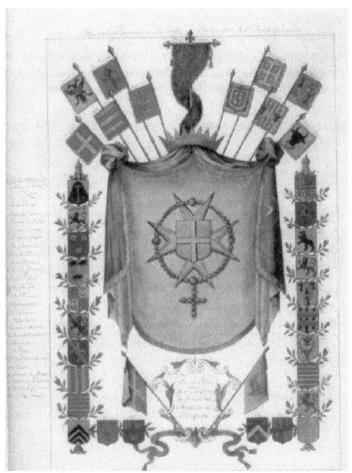

**18th century depiction of the Heraldic arms of the
late 16th century Ordre de Saint Lazare**

The depicted late 16th century arms show the simple Greek cross *vert* on an *argent* background within the escutcheon (shield). The arms are placed on the an eight-pointed cross *vert* with an *argent bordure'*. This is encircled by a beaded collar of the Order. The main arms of the Order are placed on a green-lined black mantle carrying an eight-pointed cross *vert* on the left side and surmounted by the Eastern crown. A standard showing the arms of France serves as the crest. This is bordered by five armorial flags in two rows on each side – the left showing the arms of Austria, the Holy See, Savoy, Hungary, and England; the right showing the arms of Jerusalem, Castile & Leon, Scotland, Sicily, and the Uri region in Switzerland. These represent the regions where the Order held important preceptories. Placed centrally below the mantle are two heraldic flags on each side representing the Greek cross *vert* on an *argent* background and the SLJ [**B**] initials of the Order on a *vert* background. The whole is further bordered by the family coat-of-arms of the various assumed or recorded masters up to Jean-Charles de Gayand de Monterolles [1599-1604].[29]

The amalgamation of the Order of Saint Lazarus to the Order of Our Lady of Mount Carmel in 1608 required a modification in the heraldic arms of the Order. The central escutcheon now shows the simple Greek cross *vert* of the Order of Saint Lazarus and amethyst of the Order of Our Lady of Mount Carmel on an *argent* background. The arms are placed on the an eight-pointed cross alternating *vert* and amethyst half-arms with an overall *argent bordure*'. This is encircled by the collar of the combined Orders and placed on an amethyst mantle lined with green and surmounted by the French royal crown and the French standard serving as the crest. This is bordered by five heraldic flags in two rows on each side – the left showing the Greek cross *vert* on *argent* of the OSL, the arms of France, the **M** sign on amethyst of the Order of Our Lady of Mount Carmel, the family arms of the grand masters de Nérestang and Le Tellier; the right showing the arms of Navarre and the Greek *vert*/amethyst cross on *argent* flag of the combined Orders, the family arms of the grand masters de Courcillon and Duc d'Orleans, and the flag showing the superimposed SLJ[30] initials [**B**]. The mantle has two heraldic flags on each

---

[29] In order these include: 1. Jean Horcan 2. Jean de Chypre 3. Renault 4. Gérard de Thoms 5. Boyant de Roger 6. Thomas Sainville 7. Jean de Paris 8. Adam de Veau 9. Jean de Coaraze 10. Jean le Conte 11. Jacque de Beynes 12. Pierre des Les Ruaux 13. Guillaume des Mares 14. Jean le Cornu 15. François d'Amboise 16. Agnan de Mareul 17. Claude de Mareul 18. Jean le Conti 19. Jean de Lévis 20. Blank representing Michel de Seure 21. François de Salviati 22. Armand de Clermont de Chastes 23. Hughes Catelan de Castelmore 24. Jean-Charles de Gayand de Monterolles.

[30] SLJ = Saint Lazarus of Jerusalem

side representing the arms of the Holy See and of Pope Paul V. Below, there are a further two flags depicting the two neck insignias of the two Orders placed respectively on a *vert* and amethyst background.

18th century depiction of the Heraldic arms of the 17-18th century Ordres de Saint Lazare et de Notre Dame de Mont-Carmel

The Order of Our Lady of Mount Carmel, which in 1779 had been reserved for meritorious graduates of the *École Royale Militaire*, lost its raison d'être when the establishment was closed down in 1788. The senior Order of St Lazarus however survived the vicissitudes of the French Revolution and was re-established in France during the Bourbon Restoration under Royal Protection until 1830. The latter part of the 19th century was to see the Order's protectorship being apparently assumed respectively by the Melkite Patriarchy and the Holy See. The Holy See withdrew its protectorship in 1905, and the Order of Saint Lazarus subsequently re-organized as a secular Order under the protectorship of the Melkite Patriarchy in 1910.[31]

The late 19th and early 20th century period was characterized by a neo-baroque revival that reflected itself in the heraldic developments of the restructured Order of Saint Lazarus. The modern arms of the Order were re-designed in the early 20th century on the same lines as the baroque-style one extant in the late 16th century. A depiction of the various worn insignia in use at the same time was also published.[32] The design adopted in the 1930s depicted the simple Greek cross *vert* on *argent* in the escutcheon, which is superimposed on an eight-pointed cross *vert* and surrounded by the collar of the Order. The whole is placed on a black ermine-lined mantle with an eight-pointed cross vert edged by gold on the left side. The whole is surmounted by an Eastern crown with black cap and a gold orb surmounted by an eight-pointed cross *vert*. The motto ATAVIS ET ARMIS is depicted on a scroll below the mantle.[33] A modified version was registered with the Court of Lord Lyon in 1967.[34] This led to the eventual adoption of the green cap after the re-unification of the

---

[31] Charles Savona-Ventura. *The fons honorum of the Order of Saint Lazarus: 1800-1910.* Acta Historiae Sancti Lazari Ordinis, 2019, 3: pp.65-90

[32] *La Vie Chevaleresque*, 1 July 1934, 6: pp.110-111, 117

[33] *La Vie Chevaleresque*, 1 July 1934, 6: p.117

[34] Extract of Matriculation of the Order of the Military and Hospitaller Order of Saint Lazarus of Jerusalem. Matriculated the 3rd day of August 1967. Extracted from the *35th page of the 50th Volume of the Public Resister of All Arms and Bearings in Scotland this 6th day of September 1967.*

various schismatic groups in 2006.[35] The internationalization of the Order started originally in the 1930s, but augmented in the 1960s, led to the formal establishment of a number of jurisdictions and sub-jurisdictions. All these have been assigned their own dedicated coat-of-arms showing national or regional arms in the first quarter of the international arms. Some of these have been formally registered with heraldic or trademark registers.[36]

1930s design   *1967 Lyon Court*   *Current design*
                        registration
Modern Arms of the Military & Hospitaller Order of St Lazarus of Jerusalem

Heraldic insignia of the individual members

By the end of the 14th century, the heraldic cross of the Order of Saint Lazarus started being variously incorporated in the coat-of-arms belonging to individual members. The earliest depiction of such personal coat-of-arms can be seen on the tomb effigy of Jacobi de Besnes (†1384) which are surmounted by the Greek cross, presumably green. Of note, the earlier tomb effigies of Thomas de Sainville (†1312) and Jean de Paris

---

[35] Michael Ross. *Debating the colour of the cap in the crown of the Order of Saint Lazarus: A modern detective story*. Acta Historiae Sancti Lazari Ordinis, 2019, 3: pp.135-147.

[36] For the Maltese jurisdiction registration see: Registration of Trademarks - Malta Industrial Property Registration Directorate. *Malta Government Gazette*, 8 February 2006 17877: pp.1150-1154; 1 October 2015 19480: p.13996; 18 June 2015 19442: p.10875; 4 January 2018 19930: pp.73-74

(†1349) did not include the respective family coat-of-arms. The tombstone effigies of both de Besnes and de Paris depict a dog at the feet of individual, in heraldry signifying loyalty and leadership status in the chivalric order.[37] The tomb effigy of Pierre de Pottier in the Chapel of the Commandery of St. Antoine de Grattemont (†~1480) directly incorporated the Latin cross of the Order within the escutcheon as an integral part of the de Pottier family coat-of-arms. This effigy includes the incorporation of heraldic supports in the form of angels or guardians of the dead symbolizing the spirituality of the individual.[38]

Jacobi de Besnes (†1384)   *Pierre de Pottier (†~1480)*

The personal coat-of-arms of the commander of Seedorf, Joanno de Schwarber (†~1443), incorporates the cross of the Order in a more complex fashion. The escutcheon is quartered with the Greek cross of the Order being placed in the first and fourth quarter, while the second and third depict the family coat-of-arms represented by a lion rampant. In addition, a lion rampant holding the cross of the Order surmounts the open-form mantled helmet.[39] The personal heraldic coat-of-arms

---

[37] *Tombeaux de....., op. cit.*

[38] *Épitaphe et tombeau de Potier Conflans, frère de l'Ordre de Saint-Lazare de Jérusalem, vicaire général de Des Mares, grand maître de l'Ordre, commandeur de la maison conventuelle de Boigny, près Orléans (1410), gravés par Vincent Thomassin (1700).* In: Recueil d'épitaphes, contenant de nombreux dessins de pierres tombales à la plume ou à la sanguine, avec armoiries coloriées, notes, copies et extraits de pièces. VII Mélanges. Ms. Bibliothèque nationale de France, Département des manuscrits, Clairambault 947, +72 fols.

[39] Siebert, *op. cit.*, p.102

depicted in the 16th century broadside is similarly quartered with the cross of the Order being placed in the second and third quarter, and the personal arms represented by *gules a saltire argent* placed in the first and fourth quarter.[40] Another form linking the personal arms to those of the Order was simply by linking the two arms in separate shields with a broad band as those of the Sutton family with the Order's arms as depicted at Burton Lazars.[41]

Joanno de Schwarber

Unknown 16th cent. broadside

---

[40] In a sixteenth century broadsheet related to leprosy. Reproduced in J. Harter. *Images of Medicine*. New York: Bonanza books, 1991, p.202.

[41] From notebook of William Wyrley, Rouge Croix, c.1600. Reproduced in David Marcombe. *Leper Knights - The Order of St Lazarus of Jerusalem in England, c.1150-1544*. Suffolk: Boydell Press, 2003, p.98.

Order of St Lazarus linked with Sutton family coat-of-arms

Armorial shield of Jean de Conti
superimposed on a Greek cross
(1524-1557)

Armorial shield of Jean de Lévis
superimposed on an eight-pointed
cross (1557-1564)

Another heraldic method of combining the personal arms with those of the Order involved the superimposition of the personal family arms onto the green cross of the Order. This is the form adopted in depicting the arms of the masters of the Order in the 18th century armorials of the Order. These arms clearly depict the development in cross form from the Greek green cross to the eight-pointed green cross which occurred during the latter part of the 16th century. Thus, the masters from the beginning up to Jean de Conti had their coat-of-arms superimposed over a simple cross *vert*. This cross became an eight-pointed cross *vert* after the magistracy of Jean de Lévis, i.e. after the Order started being led by individuals who were members of the Order of St John.[42]

Arms of François Michel le Tellier de Louvois
(vicaire general: 1673-1691)

Arms of Louis Stanislas Xavier de France
(grand maître: 1774-1795) [43]

Post-17th century examples of personal coat-of-arms of different grand masters of the Order of St Lazarus incised on book covers [44] and commemorative jettons [45] or published in books related to the Orders have survived. The depictions are shown either quartered with the cross of the Order alternating with the family arms of the individuals occasionally overlain over the eight-pointed cross of the Order, or simply showing the family arms superimposed on the eight-pointed cross. All the

---

[42] Thomassin, *op. cit.*

[43] Coverpage of: *Missale ordinum sancti Lazari Hierosolimitani et beatae Mariae de Monte Carmelo*. Ms., 1785.

[44] James J. Algrant y Canete & Jean de Saint Vincent de Beaugourdon. *Armorial of the Military and Hospitaller Order of St Lazarus of Jerusalem.* Delft: van den Akker, 1983.

[45] Charles Savona-Ventura. *The Sigillography and commemorative artefacts [medallions, medals, stamps, plates] of the Order of Saint Lazarus*. Grand Priory of the Maltese Islands - MHOSLJ, Malta, 2013, +55p

depictions are surmounted by the ducal crown [except one of Louis Stanislas Xavier de France which is surmounted by a *prince du sang* crown].[46]

Philippe de Courcillon de Dandeau
(grand maître: 1693-1720)
minted 1700

Louis Duc d'Orleans
(grand maître: 1720-1752)
several minted 1723-1752

Louis de France de Berry
(grand maître: 1757-1773)
minted 1757

---

[46] This is a commemorative jetton commemorating the past appointment in 1773 of Louis Stanislas Xavier de France as grand maître. He was eventually to inherit the French throne as Louis XVIII after the death of his nephew. He remained the Protector of the Order until his death in 1824.

Louis Stanislas Xavier de France
(grand maître: 1773-1814)
Minted: undated latter showing the prince du sang crown

Like their grand masters, the individual members of the Order similarly had book covers incised with their family coat-of-arms incorporating the arms of the Order either by simply overlying the family arms over the eight-pointed cross or including also the cross of the Order in an added chief. One member – Marquis Gérad Melliera – had his coat-of-arms superimposed on the eight-pointed cross depicted on a commemorative jetton minted by the City of Nantes to which he served as mayor. The majority of these depictions are surmounted by their respective crowns reflecting their status in the nobility.

Marquis Gérad Melliera (minted 1721)

Duc Daniel de Montesquiou (1681)

Bonnet de St. Leger (1720)

Comte Normand de Beaumont (1717)

Duc Abbe de Vezelay (1769)

The baroque-style heraldry was retained right up to modern times. During the organization undertaken in the 1930s, definite instructions relating to the use of heraldry within the Order of St Lazarus were published in 1933.[47] In addition, armorial certificates or brevets were issued to armigerous members of the Order. The arms used in these brevets were based on the basic design of the coat-of-arms of the Order in use during the early 20th century with the shield being replaced by a

[47] *Armoiries et Blasons - Ordnances du Grand Magistre de l'Ordre*. Délégation Magistrate, Paris: Office Central, 1933, +7p.; La Vie Chevaleresque, April-July 1938, 13: pp.90-95

cartouche with a chief depicting the Greek cross vert on argent, and the base showing the family coat-of-arms of the individual.[48]

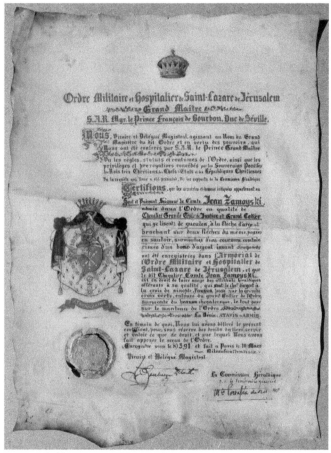

Armorial brevet No.391 made out to Count Jean Zamoyski dated 10 March 1936

---

[48] Original held by the Grand Priory of Slovakia.

Other known brevets include that made out to Prince Robert de Broglie (No. 371 dated December 1935 - published in: *La Vie Chevaleresque*, April-July 1936, 13: p.100) and to Major Alan W. Haselton (No. 416 dated 18 July 1937 – *offered for sale on e-bay* in 2015).

The role of the herald

Armorial bearings in European society became the responsibility of the appointed herald who assumed the responsibility of knowing the significance of the heraldic devices of various knights and lords, as well as the protocol governing the blazoning of arms. By the 18th century, the Order of St Lazarus assumed the practice of appointing a herald to register the members' heraldic arms. A herald or *héraut* – *roi d'armes* - *garde armorial* was appointed by the Order to maintain and update the armorial of the Order. The post was regularly filled right through the 18th century up to the last registered council in 1830 [*vide infra*].[49] The last appointed *héraut* of the *ancien regime* – Augustine-François Silvestre – died in 1851.

1725-1731	Antoine Pezey assisted by his son Pezey [*fils*]
1732-1754	Pezey [*fils*] assisted by Vincent Thomassin [in 1746-1754]
1755-1757	Vincent Thomassin
1758-1761	De Georges
1762-1774	Jean-Baptiste Duchesne
1775-1787	Ferès assisted by Augustine-François Silvestre [in 1782-1787]
1788-1791	Augustine-François Silvestre
1791-1814	Order in exile after French revolution
1814-1821	Bourbon restoration and re-organization of the Order in France
1822-1830 →†1851	Augustine-François Silvestre

List of 18th-19th century héraut – roi d'armes - garde armorial

The Herald of the Order was assigned a specific uniform. He wore a white undertunic with uncuffed sleeves, a blue jabot, black breeches, hose, and shoes. Overall, he wore a standard tabard embroidered with representations of the arms of the Order on the sleeve and front. The small cap with three feathers was worn on the head. Around the neck was

---

[49] *Almanach Royal pour l'année MDCCXXV – MDCCCXXX*. Paris, 1725-1830

the insignia of the Order on a gold chain. He carried a gold baton of office and wore a court sword.[50]

Heraut de l'ordre de Nôtre Dame de Mont-Carmel, et de S.t Lazare de Jerusalem.

The first surviving armorial pertaining to the Order of St Lazarus dates from the mid-18th century, this being prepared in manuscript form by Chevaliers Dorat de Chameulles and Vincent Thomassin. The pen and ink original has fortunately survived as is presently found in the *Bibliotheque Nationale* in Paris, France (MS Fr. 23135).[51] A second manuscript armorial in colour was produced by the same authors and is also held in the same library (MS Fr. 31795-96). These armorials depict the various blazons belonging to the various grandmasters, knights, chaplains and serving

---

[50] Pierre Hélyot & Maximilien Bullot. *Histoire des ordres monastiques, religieux et militaires, et des congregations seculieres de l'un et de l'autre sexe, qui ont été établies jusqu'à présent.* Paris: Nicolas Gosselin, 1714, volume 1, pp.257-271.
[51] *Armorial général des Ordres royaux, militaires et hospitaliers de N.-D. du Mont-Carmel et de Saint-Lazare de Jérusalem, ..., en 1753.* op. cit.

brethren up to the end of the magistracy of the Louis d'Orléans, Duc de Chartres & Orléans in 1752. No information is available about the heraldic registration regulations assumed by the Order of St Lazarus in the latter part of the 19th century.

Jean-Baptiste Duchesne
Héraut: 1762-1774

Augustine-François Silvestre
Héraut: 1775-1851

During the organization undertaken in the 1930s, an attempt was again made to introduce the compilation of armorials relevant to the Orders with formal brevets being issued to the members under the signature of *Conservateur de l'Armorial*, a post held by the Superintendent General of the Order H.E. Count Charles Otzenberger-Detaille.[52] The turmoil of the Second World War and its aftermath left the Order rather bereft of organization. The early 1960s Supreme Council does not appear to have particularly maintained the heraldic registration of the members armorial bearings. The statute governing the English Tongue promulgated in 1963 provided for the office of a Judge General of Arms and set up the Heraldic Council of the British Realms and English Tongue and South Africa. The work of the Heraldic Council was to

---

[52] *Armoiries et Blasons - Ordnances du Grand Magistre de l'Ordre.* Délégation magistrate, Paris: Office Central, 1933, +7p; La Vie Chevaleresque, April-July 1938, 13:90-95

supervise the registration of arms, the proofs of nobility, and the recording of nobiliary styles and ranks for the members within the English Tongue. The first Judge General was Sir Iain Moncreiffe of That Ilk.[53]

The post of Herald of Arms within the Order was re-instituted in 1969 when instructions were formulated regarding the design and use of the Order's armorial bearing in the armorial insignia of the members of the Order. The appointed Herald-Principal was Malcolm Innes of Edingight who also served as the Lyon Clerk of H.M. Lyon Court of Scotland.[54] The regulations relating to the use of armorial bearings in personal coat-of-arms of members were reviewed in 1979.[55] In 1982, Chev. James J. Algrant y Canete was appointed to the post of Judge of Arms.[56] Chev. Algrant, with co-author Chev. Jean de St Vincent de Beaugourdon, set out to collate an updated armorial of the Order updating the former 18th century armorials with coat-of-arms of members admitted in the subsequent decades.[57]

Sir Malcolm Innes of Edingight

[53] *Statutes, Regulations and Commands governing the Order in the Grand Bailiwick General in the British Realms and in the Commissionerate General in the English Tongue and South Africa.* Green Cross Booklet, April 1965, 6:16 21-24.

[54] *GM Decree No. 8/1969; 55/1969; & GM decree dated 15th April 1969.* In: Constitutional Decrees. Delft: MHOSLJ, 1969.

[55] *Constitutional Decrees.* Delft: MHOSLJ, 1979, 22-23.

[56] *Report of the Magistral Council held in Helsinki, Finland 7th-8th September 1982.* Finland: MHOSLJ, 1983, 5.

[57] Algrant & Beaugourdon, 1983, op. cit.

	Judge of Arms	Principal Heraldist
1969 [58]		Chev. Malcolm Innes of Edingight
1982 [59]	Chev. James J. Algrant y Canete	
1988 [60]	Chev. James J. Algrant y Canete	Chev. dr. Jorge da Silva Preto
1990 [61]	Chev. The MacCarthy Mor Chev. Denis E. Ivall [deputy]	Chev. dr. Jorge da Silva Preto
1994 [62]	Vacant Chev. Denis E. Ivall [deputy]	Chev. dr. Jorge da Silva Preto
1996-97 [63]	Chev. Denis E. Ivall [acting]	Chev. dr. Jorge da Silva Preto [resigned 1996, GM decree 6/96]
2002-04 [64]	Chev. Denis E. Ivall [emeritus: GM decree 12/2002] Don Xavier J Bastard d'Andeville [GM decree 13/2002]	

In September 1995, the Grand Magisterial Council during its meeting in Bristol confirmed, modified and approved by decision the Regulations for the recording and use of heraldry within the Order of St Lazarus. These were formally incorporated within the statutes of the Order [GM decree 26/1995].[65] These established that as an international and independent Order, the Order of St Lazarus had the ability to regulate the use of heraldry within its own jurisdiction while taking in cognizance of the different prevalent world-wide legal customs. Categories of personal arms eligible for registering with the Order included:

   a. Noble arms originating from a Sovereign or Head of a Sovereign State;

---

[58] *GM Decree No. 8/1969; 55/1969; & GM decree dated 15th April 1969.* In: *Constitutional Decrees.* Delft: MHOSLJ, 1969.

[59] *Report of the Magistral Council held in Helsinki, Finland 7th-8th September 1982.* Finland: MHOSLJ, 1983, 5.

[60] *Grand Magistral Council Meeting Vienna 1988.* Lazarus Mitteilungen, June 1988, 2A:4.

[61] *Report of the Magistral Council held in Salzburg 26th-29th October 1990.* Malta: MHOSLJ, 1990, 7.

[62] *Saint Lazarus Newsletter,* May 1994, 2:3.

[63] *Saint Lazarus Newsletter,* May 1996, 8:6; May 1997, 10:2, 4-8.

[64] *Saint Lazarus Newsletter,* May 2002, 20:4-6; January 2004, 22:2

[65] Ivall, G.E. *Report of the Deputy Judge of Arms of the Order (1995).* Saint Lazarus Newsletter, December 1995, 7:9-10

b. Burgher arms granted or assumed recognised by a competent recognised heraldic body; and

c. Assumed arms that have been in use over a period or recently adopted provided they do not infringe of the rights of others. The latter were to be relevant only within the Order.[66]

At this point the heraldic records of the Order were systematically established to include:

- the surviving ancient and updated rolls of arms reproduced in the 1983 *Ordo Sancti Lazari*;
- the Order's Golden Book comprising the arms of knights, dames or commanders who had specifically requested to be included;
- various records of arms compiled by some of the jurisdictions [e.g. Grand Priory of America] [67]; and
- informal record of arms of members extracted from miscellaneous publications but had not been formally registered with the Order.

The 2006 re-unification process bringing together the two large fractions – the Malta and Paris Obediences – necessitated a review of the statutes of the Order including the regulations pertaining to the use and registering of heraldic personal arms. These have since been modified by the decision of the Grand Magisterial Council held at Madrid in March 2012.[68]

Conclusion

The Crusader Orders originally adopted heraldic insignia to help identify the members and to serve as a rallying point on the battlefield. Heraldry took on a wider role in the subsequent centuries serving to identify and link armigerous members to the various orders. Heraldry took

---

[66] Saint Lazarus Newsletter, May 2000, 16:5-10.

[67] *An Armorial of the Grand Priory of America of the Military and Hospitaller Order of St. Lazarus of Jerusalem*. U.S.A.: MHOSLJ, 1997.

[68] *Regulations for the Recording and Use of Heraldry within the Order of St Lazarus of Jerusalem*. MHOSLJ, revised March 2012.

on a more important role during the Baroque age becoming more detailed and more closely defined. The heraldic regulations developed during the Medieval period and expanded during ~~of~~ the Baroque age were retained to modern times.

Dress Code Protocol

Abstract
A Chivalric Order requires its members to dress appropriately according to the occasion. The event may range from a highly formal occasion requiring very formal wear such as a white or black-tie events to more casual activities. The occasion will also determine the relevant insignia that should be worn.

Introduction
The activities of a chivalric order such as the Order of Saint Lazarus will require different dress codes, depending on the different circumstances occasioned by the activity one is attending. The general rules of the Order allow for a certain degree of flexibility in dress regulations acknowledging the international nature of the Order. However, it is desirable that all Members in a national Jurisdiction wear the same design in dress appropriate to the occasion. Insignia decorations and medals of the Order and other recognised national insignia may be worn on those occasions when appropriate.

Dress codes are rules pertaining to standards of attire in different social circumstances, with different rules and expectations being valid depending on circumstance and occasion. The functions of the Grand Priory of the Maltese Islands range from the very formal functions [e.g. investitures and gala dinners] to the informal casual functions [e.g. fund-raising barbecues]. A correct protocol for attire would ensure that the member is suitably dressed for the occasion.[1]

---

[1] *Dress Code Guide*. http://www.dresscodeguide.com/. A more specific reference detailed guide to dress protocol for the Military & Hospitaller Order of Saint Lazarus of Jerusalem includes: Richard Payatt, Michael Ross, & Charles Savona-Ventura. *The Handbook of the Order of Saint Lazarus*. U.S.A.: Lulu Ltd, 2nd edition, 2019, +338pp.. Also Richard Payatt. *Dressing for the Order of Saint Lazarus*. U.S.A.: Lulu Ltd, 2019, +104pp..

The uniform of the Order and the church cape should be worn only at functions and ceremonies of the Order. The members cannot wear the uniform or church capes in public functions and ceremonies. The same applies for the insignia of the Order which are intended to be worn primarily in circumstances and/or occasions associated with the Order. Where permitted by law or protocol, the insignia of the Order may also be worn on military or other service uniforms [e.g. Police Army or other uniformed volunteers].

Definitions

Badge	Distinctive device worn as a sign of membership of an Order
Bar	A strip of decorative metal added to a metal ribbon to signify a repeat award to the holder of the same decoration
Becket	A thread loop worked into the garment for the purpose of holding in position insignia brooches
Brooch	Safety pin fastening device for affixing ribbons or other insignia to the garment
Clasp	A strip of metal, wit name or date of occasion at which the holder was present, which is added to metal ribbon; similar in appearance and sometimes referred to as "bar"
Class	Degree of rank within an Order; grade
Collar	Neck chain worn over the shoulder by holders of the First Class of Orders of knighthood
Decoration	Generic term describing awards of honour, more specifically refers to insignia awarded for particular distinguished acts of bravery or service
Division	Group with an Order, usually "military" and "civil"
Emblem	Small heraldic device, usually of metal, added to a ribbon to signify or clarify the particular distinction awarded

When a member is invested in the Order, he/she is presented with:

1. The full-sized insignia of his rank, consisting of the eight-pointed cross enameled in green, suspended with a ribbon [male] or bow [female] of green watered silk. Ranks from Grand Officer and above have the insignia surmounted by a military trophy [males] or laurel wreath [females and ecclesiastics].
2. A miniature of the eight-pointed cross suspended from a ribbon [male] or bow [female] of green watered silk.

Other optional badges available include:

1. A buttonhole rosette and a miniature lapel badge with pin for males; and
2. A miniature badge mounted on a brooch for females.

The insignia, the miniature and the badge are the same object for use on different occasions and should not be worn together. The lapel badge or buttonhole rosette should never be worn with a white or black-tie dress. In addition, higher grades of the Order carry with them the breast star, the sash, the chain of office and the collar.

Dress Code

The recognised dress code for members of the Order of Saint Lazarus include:

A. **Very formal wear** --> refers to White or Black-tie events such as investitures, gala dinners, etc.

White tie Event or Full Evening: White-tie or full formal dress is actually very rare in the modern era and only normally required at Royal events, high class opera or ballet, or by the wedding party at a marriage ceremony.

a. *Male Attire*: The civilian white tie attire consists of a black tailcoat jacket with suitable trousers, full white waistcoat, wing-tipped collared dress white shirt, and white bow tie. Shoes black.

Another option on both occasions would be the use of the Gala or Mess Uniform, or a formal military or other uniform.

b. *Female Attire*: On all very formal occasions, ladies members of the Order are expected to wear a long full-skirted black dress with full sleeves normally with a décolleté neckline; evening gowns are an alternative.

c. *Decorations:* The full range of decorations should be worn during White-tie events. Where appropriate, a court sword may also be worn: ecclesiastics, women and physicians do not wear swords.

d. *Invitation* will read: "White tie, long dress — Decorations".

Gala uniform   *Mess uniform*

Black tie Event or Smoking/Dinner Jacket

a. *Male Attire*: The civilian black-tie attire corresponds to a black dinner jacket with suitable trousers [uncuffed, with one stripe on leg seams] or black lounge suit. Shirt should be stiff winged or soft folded collar with either a plain or pleated front; a black bow tie; black shoes. In common with the White tie event, another option on both occasions would be the use of the Gala or Mess Uniform, or a formal military or other uniform.

b. *Female Attire*: On all very formal occasions, ladies' members of the Order are expected to wear a long black dress; evening gowns are an alternative.

c. *Decorations:* The full range of decorations should be worn during these events. Where appropriate, a court sword may also be worn: ecclesiastics, women and physicians do not wear swords.

d. *Invitation* will read: "Black tie, long dress — Decorations".

B. **Formal wear** --> refers to Lounge suit for other social occasions.

a. *Attire*: A somber-coloured lounge suit with shirt and tie [preferably the Order's tie]. A variety of dresses can be worn by women, including cocktail dresses.

b. *Decorations:* There are very few occasions within the British and the French Realm in daytime, such as Memorial Day Services gathering, when guests are expected to wear medals with lounge suits or blazers. It is however quite acceptable at evening functions of this kind to wear miniatures [not full-sized medals]. Alternatively, a rosette may be worn in the left lapel button. No breast stars or sash, and no chain of office.

c. *Invitation* will read: "Lounge suit, short dress — Decorations" or "Lounge suit, short dress — No decorations".

C. *Business – smart casual wear*

a.   *Attire:* A suit with a collared shirt. An alternative would include a black or midnight blue blazer preferably with the embroidered arms of the Order on the left breast pocket. A white shirt with a necktie, preferably the Order's, is optional in the morning but mandatory in the evening. Trousers plain grey. Shoes plain black with black socks. During the hot summer months, a collared shirt with/out a necktie may be appropriate smart casual wear.

b.   *Decorations:* No formal decorations should be worn with this attire [no medals, neck cross, breast stars or sash, and no chain of office]. A rosette or lapel pin can be worn on the buttonhole of the jacket. No lapel pins should be worn if a blazer with the embroidered arms is worn.

c.   *Invitation* will read: "Smart casual, short dress — No decorations".

D. *Very casual wear*

a.   *Attire.* This will vary according to the circumstances of the occasion.

b.   *Decorations.* These are not suitable wear with very casual wear.

c.   *Invitation* will read: "Very casual – no decorations or insignia".

E. *Church cape events*

a. *Attire.* This will vary according to the circumstances of the occasion and may range from White tie to Lounge suit. The use of the church cape or mantle is desired and should be obligatory on all appropriate occasions. Ecclesiastical members of the Order wear the mozetta on all occasions when lay members wear the church cape. The church cape of the Order is only worn at functions and ceremonies of the Order; otherwise their wearing is prohibited. The members cannot wear the church cape in public functions without prior authorization from their respective senior officer.

b. *Decorations.* These may be worn with the mantle according to the occasion and determined by the protocol related to the mode of attire. No decoration will be worn on the cape except a single shell badge of pilgrimage on the green cross for a formal appropriately documented and approved pilgrimage to Jerusalem, Rome or Santiago de Compostela.

c. *Invitation* will read: "Black tie, long dress — Church cape – Decorations" or "Lounge suit, short dress — Church cape – Decorations" or "Smart casual, short dress – Church cape – no decorations".

Decorations Protocol

As members of a chivalric order, the members of the Order of Saint Lazarus are assigned relevant insignia according to their status within the Order's hierachy. They may also be awarded specific insignia indicating particular meritous contributions made to the Order. These insignia incude lapel medals [large and miniature], neck crosses, breast stars, and sashes. Definite protocols determine their use in various occasions.

Grade	Medal	Neck cross	Star	Sash
GCLJ	miniature		√	√
KCLJ/DCLJ/EChLJ	miniature		√	√
KLJ/DLJ/SChLJ	miniature	√	√	
CLJ/ChLJ	miniature	√		
OLJ/AChLJ	√			
MLJ	√			
GCMLJ	miniature		√	√
KMLJ/DMLJ	miniature	√	√	
CMLJ	miniature	√		
OMLJ	√			
MMLJ	√			
Medal of Merit	√			
Cross of Merit	√			
Donat Cross	miniature	√		

Insignia of the Order of Saint Lazarus

Medals

Members should wear medals reflecting only the highest class of rank or decorations. One should not wear double insignia simultaneously, e.g. a neck cross and equivalent miniature medal. The wearer must avoid a "Christmas tree effect" and wear only relevant insignia that reflect current rank and awards. Commemorative medals should NOT be worn. With civilian attire or the Gala/Mess Uniform, miniature insignia on the left lapel should be worn during evening events – full-size insignia are only worn only during morning events. Ladies should wear miniatures from a miniature ribbon bow or miniature brooch on the left-hand side of the chest. The following Orders, decorations and medals are approved for wear at the functions of the Military and Hospital Order of Saint Lazarus of Jerusalem. These should be worn in the following order, the more senior placed medially in the following order.

1. National decorations and medals awarded by a state.[2]
2. National decorations and medals awarded by other sovereign states including the Vatican [3] and the Sovereign Military Order of Malta.
3. Decorations and medals of the Military and Hospital Order of Saint Lazarus of Jerusalem.
4. Decorations and medals of the Dynastic Orders of recognised Royal and Princely Houses. [4]
5. Awards of Honours and Merit awarded by the Military and Hospital Order of Saint Lazarus of Jerusalem.

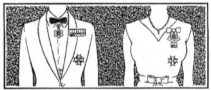

Civilian dress

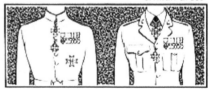

Uniform dress

Daytime Occasions with large medals   **Evening Occasions with miniature medals**

---

[2] Such as: *Malta's system of honours, awards and decorations.* https://opm.gov.mt/unuri-ghotjiet?l=1

[3] *Papal Orders of Chivalry.* http://en.wikipedia.org/wiki/Papal_Orders_of_Chivalry

[4] *Provisional List of Orders.* http://www.icocregister.org/list2001.htm

Neck decorations

Only one neck cross suspended from a full-width ribbon should be worn at any time. The ribbon should be worn under the shirt collar so that the badge rests on the tie immediately below the knot. Two neck crosses can be worn with a full formal military uniform. In this case, the senior badge suspended from its  ribbon is worn inside the collar of the tunic in such a way that the badge hangs outside with about 2.5 cm of the ribbon emerging from the opening of the collar; the second badge is worn with the ribbons emerging from the second buttonhole. Not more than one Chain of Office may be worn at any time.

Sash/Cordon insignia

Only one sash or cordon worn can be worn with civilian white or black-tie dress or the gala or mess uniform. The sash is not suitable wear with a lounge suit. The sash is worn under the jacket or tail coat over the right shoulder with the insignia cross over the left hip. When worn with the Gala uniform or in presence of Grand Master or Head of State, the sash is worn over the jacket.

Breast stars

With a black-tie civilian dress, only one Breast star may be worn on the left side of the coat. Up to four breast stars can be worn with the gala or mess uniform or with a white-tie civilian dress. Breast stars should not be worn with with a lounge suit. The Order's "Cross of Justice" is worn in a similar position as wearing one star, but it is however worn on the right side.

Wearing Breast Stars

If only one breast star is worn, it should be placed in the centre of the left breast pocket the upper point being not less than one inch [2.5 cm] below the lip of the pocket, or in the corresponding position on a garment without a breast pocket.	*
If two breast stars are worn, the second star is placed directly below the first, with its upper point being not less than one inch [2.5 cm] below the lowest point of the first star. The first star should be the senior Breast Star.	* *
If three breast stars are worn, they should be positioned in a triangular fashion with stars two and three in the horizontal line below the first star. The second star is worn closest to the chest. On occasion when the above interferes with the sash, the second star can be worn alongside the first with the latter closest to the chest and the third star below	* * *
When four stars are to be worn, they are arranged in a diamond fashion.	* * * *